GOT CLOUT?

GOT CLOUT?

The Buyers Edge

GIL JOHNSTON

iUniverse, Inc.
Bloomington

Got Clout?
The Buyers Edge

iUniverse books may be ordered through booksellers or by contacting:

iUniverse
1663 Liberty Drive
Bloomington, IN 47403
www.iuniverse.com
1-800-Authors (1-800-288-4677)

ISBN: 978-1-4620-6489-2 (sc)

Printed in the United States of America

iUniverse rev. date: 10/29/2011

CONTENTS

INTRODUCTION

It's Time to Put a Tiger in Your Corner.

Expect Changes; they are inevitable.
Engaging in the current real estate marketing scheme promoted by typical industry favorites is like playing a game of chess. Buyers are the "pawns." Sellers are the "kings", The "queens" are the typical real estate moguls dictating how the game is going to be played.

In that game, competition has always been fierce; agents scramble to see who can outbid their competitions property valuations for the right to list the sellers' property. It was a system doomed to fail. The economic misfortunes in the housing market we see today reflect that failure; it could easily have been predicted.

Tired of being the pawn? It's time to change the rules of the game under which you would prefer to play. It's your money, after all. **It's fair-play time for buyers!** Buyers get to call the shots for a change.

New rules for buyers comes with tigers in their corners. We call these tigers: **Exclusive Buyer's Brokers.** They trump the pawn brokers every day. *(Excuse the pun; it was intended.)*

If you want to get a tiger into your corner, you've picked the right book, at the right time. The acquisition of knowledge is where this game is headed. Learn the rules of the game. Get with it, or get left behind.

Dramatic Savings are headed your way! You can save thousands of dollars on your next real estate transaction. And, why not? Simply absorbing the wealth of information in this book is your first step. It's the key to your coming out on-top of the game in any acquisition. It can also put some unanticipated rewards into your pockets; that's virtually guaranteed.

Let's do an analogy: Learning how to ski has similar aspects. Would you venture out on the ski slopes without having been trained how to use your skis, or how to maneuver on the slopes? Of course, you wouldn't; although some have been known to try. A few were successful in spite of the odds.

However, you may be better off not challenging the odds. Unless experienced, becoming involved in the purchase of any real estate can be risky business. With the knowledge gained in this book and with the services of a highly qualified exclusive buyer's broker, your risks will be greatly diminished.

Knowledge and technology are what it's all about. This book provides the knowledge you may need. We will introduce you to the technology with our recommendations for your exclusive buyer's broker. You will have a very competent instructor, your broker. You can count on it. Following the guidelines provided here will put you in the driver's seat in any transaction.

However, **there is a key ingredient to your success;** an entrepreneurial spirit is essential. Warren Buffet said it: "We need innovation to get America moving again." That's where this book begins.

Warren Buffet wasn't the only prominent figure who has commented about the entrepreneurial spirit that's needed. Donald Trump reportedly expressed that sentiment more succinctly, comparing it to a football coach talking to his players: "It's time to kick butt!"

Although, "butt" may not be the precise word he used; we will let your use your own imagination. Can you imagine where our economy would be today if we had all taken that attitude seriously some time ago?

You can **begin your innovative thinking with the next real estate purchase,** or the next mortgage transaction you may undertake. Getting a good handle on the guidelines spelled out in this book would be a good place to start. You can't get much more innovative than to adopt the program recommended here. **Discover the clout that comes with that attitude and this book.**

Stand back and watch your spirits soar while your pocketbook and savings accounts become fatter!

Are We Shaking-up the Traditional Real Estate Industry?

That's certainly a good place to start: the traditional real estate marketing system is close to being broken. It has been stuck in first gear far too long. Just listen to the cries when agents proclaim, "We've always done it this way!" That's the problem.

This book and the program promoted here are a consequence of the challenges facing the industry and the nation. We think the majority of agents will prove that they are up to the challenge. The buyers will love it!

There have been some innovations in the industry in the past, but we believe they weren't moving in the right direction. Many firms embracing those familiar policies focused on listing properties. That fostered a race among agents to promote the highest prices for sellers. That merely emphasized that those quoting the highest prices usually got the listings.

No wonder the insane ensuing race for escalating prices helped bring about the collapse of the market. The system of placing arbitrarily high valuations on properties, usually merely to out-guess their competition, eventually crumbled. The markets went with it.

Today's market demands that, rather than reducing fees for the seller, **let's put the emphasis where it really belongs: providing incentives for the buyers.** In prior years, buyers rarely benefited. Our focus should be on meeting the buyer's needs; getting the best deal, saving the most money for our buyers, is where that focus should lie.

Many firms that promised the highest valuations and the lowest listing fees to sellers have gone out of business, a result of the downturn in the market. The mortgage crisis and the economic conditions that followed could have been predicted. A semblance of sanity is slowly returning to the industry, even if abruptly so in many instances.

Providing incentives for sellers doesn't cut it any longer. The purchasers are riding the crest of that wave today. In a fiercely competitive market, with lots of properties on the market, that's where it belongs. **That's where *Got Clout?* enters the picture.**

Who's Looking-out for the Buyer's Interests?

Many of the large real estate sales firms still operate on a boiler-room theory: *hire many agents and some are bound to come up with a sale now and then.* Those agents would likely scream if you were to suggest that maybe they should use some innovative ways to attract and benefit more buyers.

Buyers *"Got Clout!"* They are the innovators with an entrepreneurial spirit that should be driving the market. Following the principles described in the book can potentially profit the buyers handsomely; it may even bring more business to that broker's doors.

Ignoring these admonitions may not only be foolish for a buyer, it may mark that buyer as just another "pawn."

What's the Next Step?

Sooner or later, our readers will be looking toward buying a home, or other real estate, even if it's the second time around for them. The inherent drive to own you own home is universal. The old adage holds true: *"When it comes to land, they aren't making any more of it. Get yours while you can!"*

This book confirms the concept that knowledge is king in this world. It enables our buyers to negotiate with confidence; the best possible outcome is at stake in your real estate ventures.

Whether a first-time buyer or a veteran with one or more purchases under your belt, this book will take you there. The program advocated here provides a number of advantages over the traditional real estate acquisition process. There are numerous options for our readers. Pick and choose from those that interest you, or choose all of them. It's your move:

(1) **Financial benefits for our buyer on any real estate transaction.**
(2) **An education in becoming a knowledgeable buyer of any real estate,** including investors purchasing for future rewards. *This education can bring you a lifetime of benefits;*
(3) **Some unique ways of acquiring property** that will not only save you a bundle, but which may also put another bundle in your pocket;
(4) **Opportunities to gain considerable knowledge**—*as much or more than any real estate agent you may encounter.*

We can show you how to put that knowledge to work for your benefit without having to become a licensed real estate agent and without having to commit to spending a lot of your hard-earned money;

(5) **Additional opportunities** to turn the knowledge you will gain into more welcome incentives.

The latter are all strictly optional and require no real estate license. You can explore them, learn more about them and possibly exercise that knowledge for your benefit. Or totally ignore them if you decide that's not your "bag."

(6) **Alternatives to purchasing a home.**

These will not only save you a lot of money but may actually put additional cash in your pocket. Use these for your own home purchase or for investments in real estate, which can pay off handsomely—all without having to buy any property or to pay expensive closing costs. (See Chapter Nine.)

The Exclusive Buyers Broker

This concept is extremely important to understanding everything you will learn in this book. The **Exclusive Buyer's Broker** *(Agent, representative, etc.)* is the preferred and most highly recommended form of agency in the industry. There are many benefits that go with this kind of representation. Your broker may very well be one of them, if you follow these guidelines. That broker becomes very heavily involved in obtaining the best possible results for his or her buyers.

This book teaches certain concepts, some new and some more traditional. It will teach you everything you will need to know prior to your exercising any of these options and benefits.

However, we must first alert you to the following disclaimer:

You will be gaining information that typical real estate agents would prefer you didn't know. When they have discovered that you have read this book, you may not receive the best reception from them.

The brokers who will represent our clients are **Exclusive Buyers Brokers** *(agents, representatives, etc.)* They will expend a great deal of time and energy on your behalf in this form of representation.

Therefore, some of them may require a formal agreement between the broker and his prospective buyer prior to the broker commencing any endeavors on his or her behalf. This is common procedure with virtually all Exclusive Buyer's Representatives. This contract may be summarized as follows:

The Contract

1. **The relationship between an Exclusive Buyer's Broker and the client** may be considered, in some respects, like a partnership. Each has tasks to perform and each assists the other in fulfilling those tasks. The comparison ends there, however. In no sense of the word is it treated as a legally binding partnership.

2. **Under this unique program, the broker sponsors contributions to the buyer's costs.** The contributions come from the broker's commission earnings. Typically, the broker may contribute, for example, perhaps 50 percent of his commission, *although that is always subject to negotiations between the broker and the buyer.*

3. **The broker will also negotiate concessions from the seller** that may provide very substantial rewards to the buyer. The broker will also benefit from the negotiations. That's why there will be such great incentives for your broker to do so. *No other real estate program of which we have become aware offers this option to the buyers.*

   Concessions from the seller are always in addition to any financial incentives derived from governmental origins, or other incentives that may stem from public agencies or from lending sources. On the buyer's behalf, the broker will faithfully pursue all of these incentives with no fees charged to the buyer.

   The broker in the latter case is rewarded with a commission paid by the buyer for each concession from the seller that he or she generates, in excess of $1,000. Thus, the broker is highly motivated to get as many concessions as possible. ***That's a huge plus for the buyer, as well as the broker!***

4. Generally, the purchaser assumes the obligation to find, arrange for tours, and to **choose the properties in which he or she is interested in purchasing.** *The broker assists the purchaser, of course, in all of such tasks and will arrange the showing to his client.*

5. **Your broker wants serious buyers only.** *He doesn't want to spend his time running all over the country looking for possible properties in which you may or may not be interested. Consequently,*

he's willing to share his commission with you. On the other hand, the buyer must accept some responsibilities in order for the broker to do that.

6. **The broker writes the Purchase Offer,** along with any counter offers, as directed by his purchaser, *in the event the seller counters the offer.*

7. **The broker is responsible** for seeing that the final agreed-upon transaction documents make their way to the escrow phase for closing. But that doesn't end the broker's job. He continues to consult with his buyer and monitor the status of the closing.

The major difference between this transaction and that done through most real estate agencies is that the broker's loyalty is always strictly to his client. He has no obligation to the seller, the seller's agent. He has no obligation to the listing agency. Consequently, our broker can encourage the requesting of sizable concessions from the seller, such as a contributing to the buyer's closing costs. Getting the seller to make concessions to the buyer is our broker's specialty.

Typical real estate firms would usually not be the least bit interested in negotiating concessions from their seller. **That's where an Exclusive Buyer's Broker earns his keep.**

That's the essence of **Got *Clout?*** It's almost like a "partnership" between the buyer and his broker. The broker doesn't, however, take his license lightly. He is fully responsible for all phases of the transaction, as required by the states licensing authority, the Department of Real Estate in California.

CHAPTER ONE

Choosing and Viewing Potential Properties

This phase is of utmost importance. Your broker will lay out guidelines as to what type of home or other property you are interested in viewing in those areas of greatest interest, if you know that at this time.

Together, you and your broker will be able to define the type of property of greatest interest to you and those factors which concern you the most. You may decide what's really important, what's most desirable and what may just be a nice option, if available.

Your broker may suggest reviewing some listings on the computer in his office, or he might have you review them in your home, at your convenience. You will find most listings available on the Internet, and that may save a great deal of time In searching for properties.

You will also specify the areas, if that's known at the time, in which you would like to find a home. Your Buyer's Exclusive Agent will seek to fulfill your needs and wants. You will undoubtedly know what size home, how many bedrooms and bathrooms, etc. will meet your criteria.

He/she can print out a list of available properties that would most likely meet such criteria. They can then be viewed online initially, with follow-up visits to the properties at an appropriate time for you. You should be able to narrow your list of choices that you will likely want to view in person.

Note: From this point forward in this book, we will likely refer to all agents as "broker" or as "agent" for the purpose of simplification. Such terms will be gender neutral.

Buyers Choose the Homes They Wish to See

While driving around in areas of interest, you may see a property that looks promising. If there is a real estate sign posted, jot down some notes, such as the real estate company whose sign is posted, the agent listed on the sign, the address of the property, and, of importance, the listing agent's telephone number. Call your broker to let him know what you have discovered, if you want to pursue it further.

A box will perhaps be near the real estate sign that contains a flier and a great deal of information regarding the property. That's even better! No need to take a lot of notes.

If it's an open house, by all means don't hesitate to take the tour with any agent who may be there; *it will undoubtedly be the listing agent.* They want to sell their listings, so they will welcome you. You may want to mention that you have your own broker. They will respect this and will probably offer you a copy of their listing(s) for you to show and discuss with your broker.

Be forewarned! Many agents are aggressively seeking buyers, especially those who are unattended by a broker. Be polite. Don't hesitate to show them your broker's card if they get overly aggressive. That will usually cool them off.

But don't be put off by the aggressive demeanor. It's normal in the real estate industry. You will learn how to handle any real estate agent who you may encounter. You will find this book is an essential part of the teaching process involved in your becoming a "real estate savvy" buyer.

The market, in general, has always been fiercely competitive. Most agents will go after any unattended potential client, whenever possible. Without your broker being present, most agents will do whatever they can to latch onto you as "their" client.

You may want to advise aggressive agents that you are under contract with an Exclusive Buyer's Broker. That will certainly cool them off. The agreement with your broker provides all sorts of benefits that most agents would be unlikely to match.

It's perfectly ok to view any property with any agent. However, you may not want to mention to any agent you encounter that you have read the book.

Some agents may become uncooperative if you let on that you have read this book. Even if you were to ask an innocent question, they may turn a deaf ear in your direction. Most agents, however, will treat you with respect.

In many instances, you may be viewing the properties with the listing agent at your side. If it's an "Open House" event, such agents want to sell their listings. They will more than likely greet you with open arms, even after you have advised them that you have your own broker.

However, even then, they may still think that they might have the prospect of a new client, unless they are Exclusive Listing Agents who do nothing other than take listings. Although, they may have their buddies on the selling-side. That's whom they may want to refer you.

Call your broker for assistance whenever you have questions or need to see property that isn't on open house status. Your broker will be delighted to make arrangements to show any property to you.

If you are visiting an open house, the listing agent may be preoccupied with other potential clients and possibly with other agents. "Just looking" or "I have my own broker" may make your visit a clean approach.

It is quite possible that the listing has been taken by an Exclusive Listing Agent, and that agent will most likely be more than happy to answer your questions. They usually expect you to have your own agent. This is becoming the more common practice in those areas of the country with exclusive buyer's agents and exclusive listing agents.

If your broker isn't present, collect all the fliers on any properties in which your may have an interest. You can review them with your broker at your convenience.

Finding and Touring MLS-listed Properties

Search the Internet for listings in your preferred area. Many real estate firms will have their own websites, with their listings posted. Pick up real estate magazines that you may find in or near various shopping centers or in motels in your area. Request that they e-mail a copy of their listings to you. They will usually be happy to do so.

Be sure to note the MLS listing number that may be displayed on a For Sale sign on any property of interest. Your broker will usually be able to pull it up on his computer for review.

Note the Following: When calling a large franchise real estate firm's office, we suggest following this protocol: Do not disclose at this point that you have your own broker, **unless they are an exclusive listing office only.** The reason for this is simple. Usually the agent who answers your call will not be the listing agent, but may merely be the agent who's "on the floor" at that time.

These agents will be after your business. If they discover at that time that you have your own broker, or that you have read the book, they will likely clam up instantly and tell you to consult your own broker. If this sounds like crude behavior, it may, surprisingly, be typical with many agents you may call upon today.

When calling major real estate firms, regardless of whose listing you are calling about, the agent assigned "floor time" will be the agent who handles your call. They will expect to find a prospective client on the line.

If you just ask for the listing agent, you may be shunted aside by the agent on the floor at that time. Even then, the floor-time agents may try to tell you that they can handle your call. That's what they have been instructed to do.

Choosing the Agent is the Client's Right

It is the client's decision as to whom he or she chooses to represent them. Unless you have a contract with an Exclusive Buyers' Agent, you have the absolute right to change or discharge any agent who may have been assigned to you at any time you might wish to do so.

You can choose any agent with any firm. You are not required to have the agent who has shown you the property, nor does that agent have to be the agent who writes your offer. They don't even have to be in the same office.

Note: If you are looking for financial incentives, such as those offered by our brokers, any agent can show you the property, but your own Exclusive Buyers Broker must write the offer. That's your key to getting financial incentives and, very possibly, some great seller concessions that are generally not offered by other firms.

Engaging the Listing Agent in Question and Answer Games

They won't favor discussions such as the seller's reasons for selling. It's not the listing agent's duty to advise potential buyers of what might be pertinent facts above and beyond the normal aspects of their listings.

If they were to do so, they could be acting in the capacity of a **"dual agent"** without the express consent of their seller and without the agent having disclosed that fact to the buyer. In some states, this may be a violation of that states, Department of Real Estate regulations. It could get that agent into serious trouble as well as a potential lawsuit by the seller.

All agents are alert to the possibilities of acquiring a new client. Calling for information from the listing firm presents them with their best opportunity to get a new client.

That's why these firms go to great expense to post high quality signs. The agent who answers your call will certainly lavish great attention towards you and may even suggest that they can immediately make arrangements to show you the property.

If you are certain of your sales resistance ability, do not hesitate to view any property that any agent has listed, if you have an interest in doing so. Just be sure you let your broker know which properties you have seen as well as the listing agent's name concerning properties that interests you.

Remember: many incentives and other potential benefits are offered to you merely for being a member of the group of readers who have purchased this book. Your personal broker who has been assigned to you will go after these benefits on your behalf. Other agents, dual and listing agents, are very unlikely to match them.

Play it cool when looking at any property with any agent. You may think that's a bit like playing hardball, but that's the way the real estate game is frequently played today.

It's your right to view any property with any agent, and then decide whom you want to represent you in presenting your offer to purchase any property. However, if you are under a contract with an Exclusive Buyer's Broker, you are obligated to use that broker. All benefits you would gain from this arrangement would be lost if you failed to observe this agreement.

CHAPTER TWO

How Does This Program Work?

The Buyer's Edge Real Estate Group has expressly agreed to represent buyers under the conditions spelled out in this book. They are highly experienced and respected brokers. They have all executed contracts, committing them to all the following:

(1) The broker who may be assigned to you is known as an Exclusive Buyer's Broker. He is under a binding contract in which he has agreed to provide some great incentives to buyers who we refer to him. He also assumes the responsibility to negotiate, in many instances, healthy concessions from the seller as a condition of the sale to his buyer.

(2) These incentives are all based on formulas discussed in this book. Obviously, prices for properties will vary, as will the commissions generated from their sale. The listed prices and the commission agreements with their listing agent will correspondingly affect the incentives.

(3) Normally, the selling broker has no control over the commissions, which are usually set by the listing firms.

(4) Since commissions, when earned (on closing of the transaction), are the personal property of the broker representing the purchaser. What he does with the commissions is entirely of his choice as long as the disposition conforms to the contract executed by the buyer and the broker jointly.

(5) It is legal and appropriate that a broker representing the buyer have that authority. Said conclusions have been affirmed by the Department of Real Estate in California. We expect that they will be upheld in all states.

(6) In California, the DRE has said, "What a broker does with his own money is his business. He can give it all away if he wants." If an agent tries to tell you otherwise, it may be time to get a new agent.

(7) Our brokers choose to do this on their own volition. They will negotiate their contracts as Exclusive Buyer's Representatives with the buyers.

(8) The incentives for buyers can be all the following:

  (a) **Some very generous rebates**, sometimes up to as much as 100 percent of his broker's commissions resulting from the sales;

  (b) **Some concessions from the seller in favor of the buyer,** which are negotiated by the broker on the buyer's behalf.

The latter are, however, subject to a commission being earned by your broker based on the dollar amount of the value of the concessions. The commission is paid by the purchaser to his broker.

This is not something that the industry hasn't done in the past. Brokers often negotiate with the buyers to secure certain seller concessions. It is, perhaps, the first time it has been codified as a normal part of a broker's performance agreement with his buyer.

In most instances, it will be a modest fee and may be accounted for by reversing a portion of that part of that commission earned by the broker that is designated as payable to the buyer as the buyer's "rebate."

Concessions by the seller frequently result in reductions of the property's purchase price. In such the purchaser pays the broker's fee on the concessions by means of a reverse of that portion the sales commission being rebated to the purchaser. (This will be explained in examples.)

Suggested Commission Distributions:

We make some broad assumptions in the following estimates. Readers should be aware that the commissions earned by brokers on any transaction are always subject to negotiations by sellers and the listing brokers. There are no fixed rules governing the fees or their splits. It is, in fact, a violation of federal regulations for any group of brokers to conspire to fix fees.

(a) The gross sales commission received on any transaction, it is suggested that the broker retain 50 percent with a minimum of $1,995. The balance would be rebated to the purchaser; i.e. rebates are usually 50 percent or less, depending on the gross commission.

For example, if the commission totals $10,000, the broker would retain $5,000. The purchaser would be rebated $5,000.

(b) From the concession valued in excess of $1,000 of incidentals, it is suggested the concessions from the seller that are generated by broker negotiations, *which must all be of substantial nature not normally associated with pricing of the property,* he or she would be paid 25 percent of the negotiated gross value of the concessions.

The amount is then added to the broker's portion of the sales commission described above. This is termed a "reverse rebate."

The gross amount of the reverse rebates, along with that portion of the sales commission originally scheduled to be paid to the purchaser, cannot exceed 100 percent of the initial sales commission being paid to the broker. i.e. the broker can receive only the originally determined sales commission.

This provides a great incentive for the broker to get as many concessions as possible from the seller.

Let's see how this works out. In the previous example, the sales commission was $10,000. If your broker also negotiates a $10,000 contribution towards the buyer's closing costs, including the buyer's mortgage fees, the splits would be as follows:

Buyer initially receives $5,000 from the sales commission and he also nets approximately $7,500 from seller concession toward the buyer's costs, for a total of $12,500.

The broker nets $5,000 from the sales commission and $2,500 from the concessions, for a total of $7,500.

This part of the transaction may usually be handled in one of two ways, depending upon the negotiations:

(a) The seller may instruct the escrow officer to pay from his proceeds of the sale the $10,000 concession to the buyer. The buyer instructs escrow to pay $2,500 of that amount to the broker.

(b) The second alternative would be to reduce the sales purchase amount by $10,000.

(c) In the end, the buyer has a $10,000 reduction in the purchase price, along with $2,500 in cash from the broker's sales commission.

(d) Obviously, adjustments are made to all the figures due to the lower sales price.

Note: No commissions are due to your broker or are ever charged against any governmental grants, tax rebates or other incentives in any form from federal, state or local sources. Nor are any commissions charged against concessions negotiated by the listing agent, provided they are part of the listing contract.

Note: A reduction in the offering sales price is not considered a concession unless specifically described in the purchase agreement as such. Concessions are always itemized separately, as part of the purchase agreement and must be approved by the purchaser.

For example, If the listing agent had negotiated the concessions, and it was disclosed in the listing agreement, no commission would be due to the broker on this concession to the buyer.

Your broker works for you! Getting rebates from the sales commissions and negotiating concessions on your behalf, as well as securing available governmental grants, makes it a double win-win for the buyer. Our buyers in these situations can profit handsomely!

Disclaimer note: All commissions and concessions are subject to mutual agreement between the broker, buyer and sellers. By law, none are fixed. Those noted are all considered to be examples of our recommendations.

Brokers Follow Strict DRE Regulations

Other states will likely have similar regulations. Readers should determine the regulations that are in effect in their states concerning any suggested item in this program.

Under California Department of Real Estate regulations, at this time, there are no restrictions against any broker giving rebates from his commission to his buyer in any transaction.

Similarly, there are no restrictions prohibiting the broker being paid a commission by the buyer for negotiating concessions from the seller on the buyer's behalf.

Client-funded incentives to his broker are strictly between the client and his broker. In other states, similar rules would more than likely be applicable.

Following are some specific questions and answers posed to the California DRE

1. **Can a broker reward a buyer with rebates or other financial incentives?**
   Certainly:
   "The broker can pay his buyer his entire commission, if he wishes."

2. **Can a broker charge a commission to the purchaser on the seller concessions he has negotiated?**
   Certainly:
   Those agreements are strictly between the broker and his client.
3. **Is it ethical?**
   Of course it is:

"If a broker wants to give his money away, that's his business. If the client wants to add incentives to the broker, that's the client's business."—Direct quotes from the California DRE.

Find the Home You Want; Your Broker Takes it From There.

After reviewing the listing on the property you select, your broker will call the listing agent and discuss the property with that agent. If he needs any clarification on any aspect of the listing, or if you have any questions about the property, he will discuss those with you and with the listing agent, as needed.

Your broker may also suggest requesting a title report before making any offer to purchase the property. He would like to know the motivation of the seller for selling his property; this may sometimes be discerned in the title report. Your agent can then structure an offer correspondingly. Perhaps it is a divorce situation, or any of a number of reasons for a distress sale.

You certainly want to know that information, if possible. It can affect your offering price and other conditions. Perhaps the sellers would more than likely entertain the idea of some great concessions! That has been true in a great many situations.

Note: Short Sales and REOs *(Real Estate Owned)* are less likely to have seller concessions. Nevertheless your designated broker may be able to negotiate some concessions. This has been common. *(Banks don't like to hang onto properties they have foreclosed upon. In most circumstance, they will be open to offers!)*

Your broker will certainly want to know about your impression of the property and discuss all options of an offer with you before writing it up. Be sure to discuss the good as well as the bad aspects of the property, if any, from your viewpoint. Let your broker know of any concerns you may have about the property before progressing further. Perhaps he can get them resolved quickly.

When writing an offer to purchase, it may be tempting to ask for a good many seller concessions. However, it's wise to be prudent. Be willing to settle for less than what you may like to ask for in any offer.

On the other hand, you would be surprised at what some sellers will accept by way of concessions. If you don't ask, you will never know if it is something to which the seller might agree.

But it also has to be tempered by good judgment. This is not the time to make frivolous requests. That's where your broker's experience counts.

CHAPTER THREE

After Making the Offer to Purchase

There are three possibilities:

(1) Your purchase offer may be accepted as written. In that case the transaction will carry the signature of the seller and will require your signature acknowledging the acceptance by the seller. It will then be submitted to the escrow office designated.

(2) It may be rejected, with various reasons given, such as, another offer has just been accepted, in which case they may ask if you want to consider your offer as a backup. You can accept that. Be sure, however, that you have options to continue looking for another property. If you find another property for which you wish to submit an offer, your backup will be removed, at your request.

(3) Your offer may be countered by the seller. Or the listing agent will contact your agent for further information, possibly to request an extension of time, as her client may be out of town. Your broker will probably suggest setting a specific time frame for a response by the seller.

Listing agents will usually respect those time limits. Or the listing agent may call your agent if her client is still out of the area and they need more time to consider the offer.

The listing agent may also want to discuss the offer with your agent before countering. This is common. In the latter case, your agent will discuss the conversation with you.

Whatever the response, your agent will discuss all options with you, to come to a conclusion as to what you would like to do.

You've Got a Tiger in your Corner!

Your agent, if he is one of our Exclusive Buyers Brokers, is that tiger. Our brokers are most likely very highly experienced. When drafting an offer to purchase on your behalf, they discuss strategies with you and discuss other issues prior to completing the task.

Any offer submitted on your behalf is certain to meet your wishes. You will indicate an approval with your signature on the document.

In the offer your agent will be asking for seller concessions, all of which you will have approved beforehand; they won't necessarily be ones that the seller may be looking for, however. They usually aren't.

The agent representing the seller may suggest a counter offer, which will then be presented to your broker. The two of you will then discuss the counter. **It may come to a compromise; most transactions do.** But your broker, especially if he's one of our tigers, will protect your interests all the way.

He may suggest:

(a) Accepting a counter offer;
(b) Countering the counter offer; or
(c) Just rejecting it out-right, and perhaps he will suggest looking for another property.

Your broker would usually do the latter if he considered the counter offer by the seller was unreasonable. Keep in mind that your broker works for you, not the seller. He will suggest price, terms, seller concessions and conditions that he thinks are in your best interests.

Remember, it's Always your Decision.

While your broker will provide recommendations that he thinks are in your best interests, the decisions will always be yours to make. Your broker is your mentor; his measure of success will be in the negotiations on your behalf and the savings and benefits he will be able to chalk up for you.

You will never be under any pressure to accept a counter offer. In typical situations with typical real estate agents, you never know if the agent is pressuring you to accept a counter offer because of the commission that's at stake for that agent, or if he is seriously looking after your interests.

You can rest assured that the Buyers Exclusive Representative, your broker, is looking entirely and solely after your interests.

CHAPTER FOUR

An Abundance of Benefits for our Purchasers

The benefits for our purchasers are defined in this book and in the contracts for **Exclusive Buyers Representation** made between the purchasers and their brokers. This book and our brokers will teach their purchasers all the procedures recommended for finding, making tours of these properties and making the **Offer to Purchase** at the appropriate time through your broker.

A subscribing member is defined as anyone who has purchased a copy of this book and has entered into an **Exclusive Buyer's Representative contract** for the services of one of our approved brokers.

After the member has selected a property they are interested in purchasing. the broker prepares all necessary documentation. The broker is responsible for securing the buyer's signatures on the offers and for the submission to the listing agent. Your broker is always in compliance with his broker's licensing laws in the state in which he or she is practicing.

All earnest-money deposit checks that accompany the offers are usually made payable to the escrow company, or an attorney, if an attorney is handling the transaction, or as otherwise may be dictated by the laws of the state in which the broker is licensed.

The earnest-money deposit checks are usually in the form of personal checks from the party making the offer. They may also be cashier's checks from the purchaser's bank.

No earnest money deposits should ever to be made payable to any real estate broker or to your broker's company, unless your broker maintains a trust account for that purpose. He or she will advise you as to how to make the deposit check payable. Never make a check payable to the property owner. even if you are negotiating your own purchase transaction.

The suggested amount of a deposit on the initial offer is between $500.00 and $1,000 for most properties. The exception may be for properties that are priced over $200,000, or whatever amount is generally customary in the states in which the broker is licensed. The broker will suggest the amount of the earnest money deposit, and to which escrow office or attorney.

The rationale for making minimal deposit checks is that you don't want to tie up your funds on an offer that involves extensive time for closing. The seller or the seller's agent can request a higher figure if that is necessary to make them feel comfortable with your offer.

From a legal standpoint, the offer is valid no matter how small the deposit. However, some agents and some sellers may get "uptight" if they don't think the deposit is large enough to indicate a sincere offer.

Earnest money checks are <u>never</u> made payable to "cash." They should always be held by the real estate broker until the buyer and seller have agreed to all terms and conditions and have signed all offers and counter offers. Only then does the transaction advance to the escrow stage, where the deposit check is then presented to the escrow firm, or attorney if one is involved. A deposit

The broker representing the purchaser will deliver the original of all properly executed contracts between the parties to the escrow office or to the attorney handling the transaction, along with the earnest money deposit if that is appropriate. Your agent will advise you, when preparing your check to the firm or attorney to which the earnest money check should be made.

In many parts of the country, both title and escrow functions are handled by a single firm. In other parts of the country, they may be handled in a different manner, especially if an attorney is involved.

Your broker will schedule all consultations with his buyers to discuss properties in which they may be interested. He or she will discuss all facets of any offers. The consultations are always free of any charge. The exceptions may occur if a buyer is representing himself in a transaction. He or she may merely securing advice and assistance in drafting documents. In the later case a broker would be justified in charging for advice and for preparing any documents.

Neither your broker nor the seller's broker is ever paid until the escrow office or attorney closes the transaction; nor are the listing office and the selling office ever entitled to any fees until the closing of the transaction. The only exception to the rule would be an instance in which the broker is merely providing advice and preparation of documents. The broker in the latter instance would be paid by the buyer regardless of the completion of the sale. Some brokers are happy to work under such terms.

Eligibility for Participation in the Program

Participation in the program is extended to all purchasers of *Got Clout?* The knowledge contained in the book is critical to all participating members of the elite group of readers.

Our brokers rely on their purchasers having this knowledge prior to executing contracts to purchase property. In order to participate, readers may be required to execute contracts for Exclusive Buyers Representation prior to your assigned broker providing any services. It's a relatively simple contract and contains sections confirming all the benefits listed here.

All benefits included in the book are provided at no cost to the participating members of the elite group. After purchase of the book there is no requirement for membership in any organization.

Additional benefits and incentives may be added from time to time. Benefits include free consultation on all your real estate matters with one of our brokers. Our websites is an excellent means of keeping up to date on all issues affecting buyers and the market. The website may also discuss special opportunities of interest to our membership.

Legal Advice is Never Provided by Brokers

Neither we, nor the brokers participating in the program, provide any legal advice on any matter other than that required to complete standard real estate contracts or other commonly used forms. They can, of course, provide consultation and advice on real estate properties and matters of their professional license.

If any state in which this book is sold requires standard forms to be completed by an attorney, we advise our readers to follow the rules and regulations of their state. However, if any reader has questions regarding real estate matters, they are welcome to discuss them with any of our brokers. The broker will be able to advise you if he thinks you should consult an attorney.

However, no restrictions exist in any state that a purchaser making an offer to purchase be required to use an attorney or a real estate agent if the purchaser wants to complete the forms himself and handle his or her own transaction.

Who is Eligible for the Benefits?

All members of the general public are welcome to take advantage of the services provided. The only requirement is that they have purchased and have read this book, *Got Clout?*

Options for consultation on other types of real estate investments are also available to our reader/members. Our brokers will be happy to discuss any issues and options to acquire any real estate, regardless of where or what it may be. Talk it over with the experts before making any moves that may not get you the most value for your money!

Pick and Choose the Benefits You Want

(1) Rebates on your own purchases can save you a bundle.

Your home purchases can result in substantial savings with the rebates to which you will be entitled. Rebates, in many instances, may total thousands of dollars. The disbursals can be applied to your closing costs, your down payment, or just put into your pocket upon close of escrow.

*Note: Listing offices always set the commissions to be paid by the seller on their transactions. Our brokerage firms normally have no control over such figures.

Do we have any leverage with the listing office? Yes, there are tactics that can be followed in the latter instance. They will be discussed with our purchasers at the time such an issue arises.

(2) (2) Seller Concessions:

Potentially, additional thousands of dollars from seller concessions may result from your broker's negotiations with the seller or the seller's agent when presenting your offer to purchase any property.

Our brokers are skilled negotiators. They excel at extracting concessions from the sellers. This is one of the many benefits our brokers have over typical real estate firms that may represent the seller rather than the buyer.

Your broker will be an Exclusive Buyer's Agent. These agents normally represent purchasers only. They owe no loyalty to the seller, to the seller's listing agent or to the listing firm.

Think about it: Why would an agent representing the seller want to suggest making concessions to the buyer? Obviously these may not be in the seller's interests.

Your agent, on the other hand, can increase his or her share of the commission earnings through this process. Wow! What an incentive for the buyer and his broker.

The broker gets a minimal commission from the buyer for negotiating the concessions from the seller. The maximum fee the broker can earn from the concessions, however, may not normally exceed the total amount of the sales commissions originally stipulated in the listing agreement.

On the other hand, this gives your broker great incentives to push for as many concessions as possible. And that may make it very profitable for his buyer.

(3) Assistance in obtaining the best mortgage financing under the best terms possible. Online newsletters will keep you posted. We continue to negotiate with lenders through our resources with top lenders willing to give concessions to our reader/members.

(4) Mentoring benefits:

You may want to become a mentor to your buddies and their friends. The mentoring process is strictly optional, however.

A firm that specializes in the mentoring process will provide compensation for those who wish to become mentors specializing in teaching others about the program. Your brokers may contribute part of their commissions to the mentoring firm.

In that instance, the broker's contributions come strictly out of his own pocked, and not from the buyer's pocket. If interested, talk to your broker about becoming a mentor. The mentoring benefits are in no sense of the word called referral fees. They are strictly payment for your engaging in the teaching process.

Of course, the benefits are always subject to the Department of Real Estate in California and in other states. However, these benefits would rarely come under the jurisdiction of the real estate department in any state.

A mentor may earn as much as $500, or more, for teaching friends and fellow employees about Got Clout? No real estate license is required. Teaching experience would be a plus factor.

Firms outside your state may be involved in the teaching process. Let us know if you are interested. We will pass the word on.

(5) Additional rebates and other incentives under governmental or lender programs may be available to all purchasers and are always over and above the rewards noted above.

No commissions are ever charged the buyer on any government, lender, or quasi-governmental incentives to buyers!

(6) Want to learn about investments in real estate?

You can, strictly at your option, learn about investments in real estate. Discover, for example, how to create an investment group, or how to syndicate real estate acquisitions.

You can participate with others, do your own, or stand back and just observe. No real estate license is required for participants. No fees are charged for any consultations. Your broker is ready to do the mentoring.

For example, suppose you and some buddies want to purchase a mobile home park along the Oregon coast. Each of you takes a few weeks in the summer managing and doing maintenance.

You've all just created a tax deductible working vacation that covers all travel and living expenses incurred in getting there, staying there and returning from there. Take your families along and put them on your payroll.

Of course, your accountant would prefer you didn't refer to it as a vacation. Obviously it would have to meet IRS regulations. Just be sure you have a good accountant. The Oregon coast is absolutely delightful in the summer, and at other times of the year!

(7) How to Profit From the Lease-Option:

You can profit from real estate without ever owning the property and without having to put down large sums of money. Nor are there any loan fees or closing costs, unless and until you decide to exercise your option to purchase the property and you intend to finance it.

But if you are in it strictly for profit, you can, and many do, contract for a lease-option property without ever actually closing any transaction to purchase the property or to put a loan on it. You can fix it up and put it back on the market before your option expires; and in many cases, make a nice profit.

It's a good way to perhaps acquire your first home. The experts do it all the time. Our brokers will teach you how you can profit from the lease-option and when it's in your best interest to do them. Our online newsletters will, from time to time, will discuss opportunities to participate is such groups.

The broker's consultation is free to our members. All it takes to become a member of this fraternity of smart buyers is the purchase of the book: ***Got Clout?*** Of course, your participation in any of these options is strictly your choice. Pick and choose what you want to do. They are all included when you become involved in the programs suggested in the book.

Getting rebates, seller concessions on your purchases and even mentoring others can easily add up to thousands of welcome dollars. You can count on your broker looking after your interests. For further information and instructions for creating a lease and/or option offer, see the Lease-Option; Chapter Nine.

CHAPTER FIVE

How to Get Paid for Initiating Your Own Purchase

Let's begin this chapter by making some assumptions:

(a) You are intent upon spending your money wisely in any real estate transaction in which you are the purchaser;
(b) You want the best value, the best investment and the most seller concessions, with the lowest purchase price;
(c) Obviously, you don't want the services of an agent who has his seller's interest in mind. If you are looking for that kind of representation, you may well come in second or even third best under such circumstances.

The brokers we contract with are Exclusive Buyers Representatives. Your interests, not the seller's interests, are their primary concern.

If these assumptions meet your specifications as a potential home buyer, you are on the right track, in the right place and at the right time in your search for a property to buy. You will find these instructions always get to the point—no pussy-footing around, no platitudes, no painting of rosy pictures—just common sense.

This book teaches the fundamentals of buying real estate while saving money. You want to go away from your real estate experiences with a satisfied smile on your face: You don't want to end up wondering whether you got a good deal. It also discusses some of the pitfalls to avoid in any real estate or mortgage transaction.

Some Conceptions and Misconceptions

There are some fundamental facts relating to the real estate industry with which you need to become familiar. These need to be understood by purchasers before proceeding down the path to buying any real estate.

There are three general categories of real estate agents you may encounter in this industry:

(a) Selling Agents:

Some of them may be known as **Exclusive Buyer's (Brokers, Representatives, etc.).** Usually, the latter represent buyers only and usually do not take listings. The real estate brokers and their agents represented by this book are Exclusive Buyers Agents.

You can be certain they will represent your interests exclusively; not the interests of the sellers, not the seller's agent nor the listing company. If there are any conflicts of interest, agents are obligated to inform you at the outset so that you can make an informed decision as to whether you want to be represented by an agent that represents the seller, or one who represents the buyer exclusively.

Remember that you have the right to select your own agent. Your first step should be to determine who that agent is representing: the seller, the buyer, or both seller and buyer.

(b) Listing Agents:

Some of the agents may exclusively represent only sellers, or may primarily represent sellers. They may or may not represent the buyer, too, in which case they would be acting as dual agents.

(c) Dual Agents;

Those agencies represent both buyer and seller. It's the most common form of agency in much of the country. If not understood, it may be the riskiest form of agency you may encounter.

If you do end up with this kind of representation, be sure you have an open and frank discussion with the agent; you want to know under what rules you will be playing should they want to show you a property for which they, or another agent in their office, may be the listing agent.

A dual agency representative may immediately give rise to a conflict of interest in which you may easily come in second or even third best in any such transaction. The real estate laws in many states stipulate that agents must give you notice if they are acting as dual agents.

Ralph Nader once criticized the dual agency concept used by so many real estate firms as the worst form of representation you can have.

Two Basic Types of Licensees

(a) Brokers who can also act as agents, and
(b) Agents working under a contract with a broker.

While each can be an "agent" in a typical transaction, only the broker has the power to make crucial decisions. The typical agent *(nonbroker)* is often virtually powerless to make the kinds of decisions which can be very important to the buyer.

However, the broker can give his agent the authority to make such decisions for him, subject to the broker's oversight.

An agent other than a broker usually has a smaller piece of the pie that she or he can earn as a commission, and hence a smaller piece of the pie that he or she can offer to share with a buyer, if that subject were to arise. Some agents would likely be flustered if confronted with a suggestion by the buyer that she pay the buyer a piece of their pie. Only the broker can make or approve such decisions.

However, brokers can and do make such arrangements with their agents who have shown the capabilities of performing in the way the broker sees it being performed. Those agents may be, and often are, the exception. It requires discipline and loyalty to their broker as well as the broker's full consent for that agent to act in lieu of the broker.

In most states, agents are required to be under contract with their brokers as "independent contractors." They are usually not classified as employees. Broker-Agent contracts go to great lengths to make this distinction between employee and independent contractor very clear.

Noted here are some of the actions and responsibilities agents can be authorized to do:

1. Agents can become "managers" of a real estate office, usually with two years or more of full-time experience, but only when empowered by their broker to do so.
2. Agents, unless empowered to do so by their broker, cannot negotiate commission splits with other agents and/or with sellers or buyers except with the broker's acknowledgment; Brokers, exclusively, have this power.
3. Agents can become brokers, usually after two years full-time experience in most states, by passing additional real estate courses and examinations. The courses must meet the approval of the department of real estate in that particular state.

Not all brokers like to work for themselves. Many prefer to work out of other brokerage offices. Brokers can work for more than one firm and at the same time. For example, they can work for their own firms as well as firms owned by others. A broker working for another broker is known as an Associate Broker.

Associate brokers have been known to work with or under nonbroker agents who are employed by another broker to run that particular office.

Agents *(nonbrokers)*, unlike brokers, can work only for or under one broker at a time.

Some Questions and Answers

(a) Can an agent negotiate a rebate to a purchaser on a commission being earned on a sale by that agent without the broker's permission? And, can the agent negotiate commission splits with another agent?

In both instances the answer is: "Not unless authorized by the broker to do so." Most brokers reserve that power to themselves. Other brokers can and do allow their experienced agents to do so under their supervision.

(b) Is it legal to rebate a part of the commission being earned by the broker to a non-licensed buyer who is purchasing a property through that broker?

Yes, unless specifically disallowed by the laws of the state in which the broker is licensed. The following may be a touchy subject with the departments of real estate in various states:

The general rule is that brokers cannot pay referral fees. However, Brokers can pay a third party to do training and other tasks, provided there is no relationship to a "commission" when being paid to a non licensed individual.

The Department of Real Estate in most states always has the right of approval or disapproval of these fees with respect to their real estate laws and their brokers.

(c) Can a broker pay a "finder's fee" or a "referral fee" to an unlicensed individual?

The qualified answer is: "No." Paying a "commission" to an unlicensed individual is strictly prohibited.

Certainly, the term "referral fee," as applied to the agent seeking a referral fee from or to any number of other agencies—such as title and escrow firms, pest inspectors, etc—would clearly be a violation of the DRE rules and regulations in most states.

(d) Can a broker represent a buyer purchasing a property anywhere in the state in which the broker is licensed?

Certainly, in most states, the broker can also give the authority to his agents.

CHAPTER SIX

Listing and Selling Commissions vs. Seller Concessions

Normally, the gross commission is split between the listing firm and the selling firm. Sometimes the same firm does both the listing and the sales. They make a double commission when doing so. They would be acting as "dual agencies" in those instances.

Traditionally, the seller contracts with the listing agency to pay the gross commission to that firm. The split between listing and selling agencies will usually be 50/50.

However, the MLS services have no authority to set fees, commissions or to otherwise stipulate how they are to be split or how much the fee should be. To do so would be violating anti-trust laws.

Commission rates vary from company to company. It also varies with the selling price of the property. Three percent has traditionally been customary for the selling firm and for the listing firm. However, there are no regulations anywhere in the country governing commission fees or their splits between offices.

Seller concessions are not traditionally treated as commissionable. Consequently, few agents gave much thought to getting the sellers to grant many concessions to their buyer, except when shrewd buyers, and sometimes their agents, brought up the subject. Some listing agents used "concessions" by the seller to induce quicker sales. In some instances, buyers were known to select the own exclusive buyers agent to represent them in a transaction and frequently offered their agent a bonus for that agent's performance in getting what the purchaser wanted.

We have decided to formalize the tradition and make it part of the Exclusive Buyer's Agents services that could be commissionable in the buyer's position. This creates a favorable and very desirable attitude by the buyer's agent to strive for as many concessions from the sellers as practical. This concept has been incorporated into the Got Clout? program. It's a win-win situation for both the buyer and the buyer's agent.

Since our buyers are getting a piece of the broker's commission, it is only fair that the broker have a means of obtaining a full commission, or close to a full commission, after conceding part of his sales commission to his buyer.

It's been said, "All is fair in love and war." We think that's true when a broker represents a buyer as that buyer's exclusive agent. The broker needs intense dedication in getting his buyer the best possible result from any transaction. And he deserves proper compensation. Sellers have their own agents who are attempting the same for their sellers. And some sellers often grant comparable bonuses to their listing agents. Buyers are entitled to have agents who "go to bat" for their buyers. **Got Clout?** does that.

Seller Concessions

Under our recommended program, the broker also receives 25 percent of all additional savings resulting from concessions the broker has negotiated with the seller. This is, of course, negotiable between the broker and his buyer, as are all commissions between sellers and their listing agents.

Generally, this arrangement favors a broker who aggressively negotiates seller concessions for his buyer. We emphasize the word "aggressively." That broker will work very hard getting top dollars in concessions for his buyer from the seller.

Under this arrangement, our purchaser does exceptionally well from his or her 75 Percent of the concessions plus a share of the broker's sales commission.

Note: Minor concessions, such as the seller throwing in some appliances, do not come under these concession agreements. Usually the concessions covered are those that exceed certain minimums of, perhaps, $1,000, or more. They are frequently related to lump-sum contributions by the seller toward the buyer's closing costs. However, they can cover anything that the buyer and his Exclusive Buyers Broker jointly agree to. There are no written rules. Buyers and their brokers make their own deals, which will be spelled out in their contracts for service. (See Chapter two for a review.)

Very few real estate firms would gain anything from the concessions they negotiate and would not pay anything to their agents for the negotiating of concessions from the sellers.

It pays to do business with our Exclusive Buyers Brokers. Most agents have no incentive to go after any concessions. It's a win-win situation for our buyer. The buyer makes a handsome profit from each concession negotiated by the broker.

Another Scenario

Let's assume another scenario. In the first example discussed in Chapter Two, with a sale price of $250,000, the government is also offering the first time homebuyer a tax credit of up to 8,000. The seller's agent is also promoting a three percent seller contribution to the purchaser's costs.

That's a total of $15,500. Since none of the concessions were promoted by the selling broker for the purchaser, he gains nothing from them other than the satisfaction of seeing his buyer get a great deal.

But add to that the portion of the sales commission that is rebated to the buyer. The total now reaches $19,250 in seller negotiated concessions and your broker's commission rebate.

A Worse Case Scenario

If the sale price were only $100,000, with a gross sales commission of $3,000: Let's say they split the commission: the broker collects $1,500 and the buyer gets $1,500. If the broker also negotiates a concession of, say, $5,000, from the seller at the same time, the buyer's share would be $3,750 plus $1,500 from the commission equals $5,250, well in excess of 100 percent of the entire selling commission.

The broker would have received $2,750, which amount to almost a full commission if the broker were to receive all of it. If the broker had a sales agent handling the transaction, the broker would have realized a very small portion of the commission. It is apparent that this arrangement is profitable for both the buyer and the broker.

There could be some minor reductions in the gross commission in all these examples. These corrections and the reduced commission will affect the seller's expenses of the sale, which will be accounted for by the escrow office at closing. The examples quoted here are only hypothetical. Your broker can quickly and easily give his buyer comparisons in any given situation.

CHAPTER SEVEN

The Financial Side of Your Purchase

Two primary factors affect mortgage loan qualification:

(1) Credit History:

Lenders look carefully at your past credit history in determining the risk factor in making a loan. Under normal conditions, for most lending procedures, the higher the risk factor for the lender, and the higher the interest rate. Correspondingly, a higher down payment may be required, and that may affect your monthly payments.

If you want the best interest rates, be prepared to have a good credit history, with no late mortgage or rent payments; and stellar credit, with all other accounts in at least the past two years.

That means no bankruptcies in the preceding two to four years. A bankruptcy will actually show up on your credit report for a period of ten years from the date the bankruptcy was finalized.

All other credit should also be good. Even one thirty-day late payment can be troubling. You better have a good explanation. It probably won't hurt provided your explanation is sound. More than that, however, will require some very good explanations.

Credit reports are always subject to error. Getting reporting errors removed may sometimes require considerable effort and time. For that reason, you should allow ample time for getting all your ducks in a row before starting to look for a home to buy. Getting prequalified well in advance is critically important.

(2) Income and Income stability:

During the prequalifying process, a loan officer will look at the ratios you present to a lender. The ratio of your income, compared to the sum of the mortgage payments, plus taxes, plus insurance, plus home owner's association fees and other debts should conform to traditional guidelines in order to qualify for a conventional loan.

These ratios are generally referred to as the front end and back end (sometimes called top and bottom), which are defined as follows:

(a) The Front End Ratio

This ratio is formed by taking the sum of the monthly payments on the loan, plus the monthly share of taxes, hazard insurance, mortgage insurance if any, and homeowner's dues, if any. This is known as **PITI** (principal, interest, taxes, insurance,) the sum of which is divided by your gross monthly income.

"Gross" means before taking out any income taxes or other deductions. Generally, with a 20 percent down payment, the front end ratio should not exceed 33 percent, although there are exceptions.

(b) The Back end Ratio:

The back end ratios are defined by adding all your other monthly obligations to PITI (see above). These may be payments on credit-card debts, car payments, payments on a second home mortgages, alimony or child support and other obligations expressed in monthly payment terms. Furniture and appliances purchased on time contracts would be good examples.

This is calculated as follows:

(3) Add up all your credit card debt plus revolving accounts, such as Sears or Penney's, and take 5 percent of that amount.
(4) Add that 5 percent to your car payments and any other fixed contract payments expressed as monthly payments.
(5) Add alimony and child support payments, *again expressed in monthly terms.*
(6) Then add PITI (calculated above) to this figure.
(7) Then divide that total sum by your gross monthly income to determine your back-end ratio. This should not exceed 38 percent for the loans, with the best interest rate.

That's only a 5 percent leeway between the front-end and the back-end ratios. Don't expect favorable treatment if you are pushing these ratios. Think about seriously reducing your debt before thinking about buying a home.

Any lender can provide an accurate estimate of your closing costs—known as a GFE (Good Faith Estimate). A loan officer at any lending institution can show you comparison charts that will provide various loan scenarios, with their respective estimated fees.

Your Credit—the Good and the Bad

Major credit bureaus may use what is known as FICO scoring. These are scores determined by a computer program which factors in a number of elements.

These may include:

(a) The amount of credit you have had and by how much your current credit balance represents more than 50 percent of the most credit each individual creditor on each account has granted to you. Some lenders are now eyeing 35 percent as the critical level.
(b) Late payments on mortgages and to other credit issuers;
(c) Bankruptcies within the past ten years; the previous two to four years is critical.

(d) Liens, judgments and collections;

(e) Foreclosures on previous mortgages;

(f) Repossessions of automobiles, boats, private aircraft and other large equipment purchases;

(g) Other credit issues that may be a factor in determining whether or not you will be approved for a loan. Are you current, for instance, on child support payments for which you may be committed?

(h) The number of credit requests you have made within the past 12 months, and by whom, can be a factor;

(i) The number of creditor's inquiries you have had in the past 12 months may be very important.

Credit Bureau Reports

Some studies have shown that credit bureaus report accurately less often than you might suspect. It is possible that less than 60 percent of the reports are accurate. That's better than the 50 percent that used to be common. There have been major attempts to improve accuracy even further.

FICO scores were designed by the Fair-Isaacs Company, hence the acronym FICO, as a computer-originated scoring program that arbitrarily uses a point system to evaluate your credit status. Along with lots of criticism about the system, there have been attempts to improve its performance.

Credit bureaus usually look for three or more reporting creditors in order to evaluate your credit. These should have been consistent for the past 24 to 36 months. A few recently opened accounts that have been seasoned for only a six-month period won't go far. Less than six months, it probably won't be factored into the scores.

If you think an error has been made by a creditor, be sure to compile your evidence of the error, *such as canceled checks, copies of money orders, etc.* Then write a letter to each of the three reporting bureaus detailing your findings.

By law, they are required to remove that rating for a period of up to 30 days. During that 30-day period, they can reinstate the information, provided they have verified their findings.

Usually, it will turn out to be an error by the reporting company; rarely an error by the credit bureaus. If they cannot find reasonable evidence to restate their findings on your credit report, they must permanently remove that item.

Be sure you send copies to all three reporting agencies, if necessary. Often, however, one or two bureaus may have corrected it and only one is reporting in error. You need only send your letter to those reporting in error.

If you have any questions about your credit reports, your loan officer at your lending firm should be able to consult with you and assist in removing errors. If they refuse to provide you with assistance, you may want to consider taking your loan elsewhere.

Search the Internet to determine the current addresses of the bureaus and also their telephone numbers so that you can call. Don't be put off if you call and get an unsympathetic response. These are all private agencies with, as some callers have stated, a tendency to put all callers down. They do not like being challenged. However, they are by no means infallible, in spite of what they would like you to believe.

To their credit, some of the reporting bureaus have been trying to improve their tarnished images. If you contact an employee at any bureau, be polite and friendly (they have been subject to abuse by callers as well,) but be persistent. Clearly state the reasons for you call. Be explicit. Remember, they are busy too.

CHAPTER EIGHT

Looking for a Mortgage with Less than 20 percent Down?

Not surprisingly, several such loans are available. You may still qualify for some great rates, even though you don't have 20 percent in cash for the down payment, as long as you have ample reserves, usually about six months or more, in the bank to cover those monthly payments.

You may be able to obtain an FHA loan for 97 percent or even 100 percent financing; a great credit history is not required. It helps if you have a solid employment record with adequate income and reserves.

It is frequently possible to get the seller to contribute $5,000 or more to your closing costs. Some real estate firms are pushing such loans on their buyers, by getting the buyer to agree to add that extra $5,000 to your purchase price instead of asking their sellers to contribute that amount.

That's another instance in which it pays to have an **Exclusive Buyers Broker** looking after you. They would be after the seller or the seller's agent to pony up that extra sum. In the latter event, even your broker may contribute. It never hurts to ask!

Be forewarned that some lenders pushing the FHA loans may be loading you down with extra fees! Make sure you shop for more than one FHA lender if you are in that market.

The FHA program may possibly be faulty in a number of respects. It may take no effort to protect the buyer from substandard, and sometimes very shoddy, construction. Relying on your typical real estate agent to inspect the property may be far from being adequate.

FHA may not care, for example, if the windows have up-to-date construction or are just single-pane, and that can be costly when it comes to paying heating bills.

If you are considering purchasing any home, whether it is an FHA loan or other type of a loan, be sure you have a licensed home inspection firm provide you with a written inspection report.

There may be other features in the home that aren't up to date as far as the building code is concerned. FHA standards are minimal; that may not be satisfactory for you.

Look for USDA Loans in Rural or Semirural Areas

As long as Congress continues to fund the programs, they can be a great choice, particularly for rural areas with lower income families. This means towns or small cities located in an agricultural area with a population of less than 25,000. You may qualify for a USDA (United States Department of Agriculture) loan with 100 percent financing.

You should have at least two years in current employment, unless you can show upward mobility in the job market. This means that you're in the same, or perhaps closely related, line of work, or an upward extension thereof.

Lenders will be looking for job stability. If you have moved to a better paying job but in a different line of work, be prepared to show a history in that previous job category for at least the previous two years, with reasonable credit scores.

Some employment, such as the teaching profession frequently comes with "tenure." Teachers are generally excellent prospects for mortgages and home purchases. (The current economic crisis may be an exception.)

Certain areas can be losing population of a certain age range. Schools begin closing in those circumstances. Teachers are accustomed, however, to the need to be mobile in looking for stable or growing school districts.

There is often a greater turnover of the teaching population in areas that are less stable. Teachers new to the profession often take jobs in those areas to gain experience, and then move on to more stable areas as they gain experience.

Often, they do not remain in those areas long enough to consider purchasing homes there. That doesn't mean they don't look for homes in other areas from which they can commute to the schools where they teach. Some school districts may be more restrictive in hiring teachers who don't live in the area where they will be teaching.

The Effects of a Bankruptcy on Your Credit History

Normally, a bankruptcy will remain on your credit report for ten years. A recent bankruptcy, however, may not necessarily prevent you from getting a mortgage loan approval. It will, perhaps, cost you a higher interest rate, as the lender considers this a higher risk factor to a loan. The higher the risk, the higher the interest rate you can expect to pay.

However, this does seem to contradict common sense in defining what constitutes a "risk factor." Since a recent bankruptcy affects only your past credit history, a lender or credit provider knows that your debts cannot be subject to further bankruptcies for at least 10 years.

By that time, mortgage liens under normal circumstances will have built up a reasonable equity for the purchaser, assuming no secondary liens have been placed on the property, or that the market is not declining.

And that does enter the willingness of many lenders to consider granting a mortgage at good rates. To be on the safe side, be sure to present a credit score that reflects good credit for the previous two years, along with job stability.

Prior to the mortgage meltdown era, many borrowers were lured into buying properties they normally could not afford. Initial offers by lenders for low payments and an artificially low interest rate made it extremely easy for otherwise unqualified buyers to purchase properties they couldn't afford under normal circumstances. That's why such loans may have been called "subprime".

These loans made it easy for virtually any buyer to speculate that the property they were purchasing would rise rapidly in value, even if the "value" was becoming artificially determined. The buyers assumed they could turn the properties and make a nice profit before the interest rates and their payments edged upward. (in retrospect, perhaps "leaped upward" would be a better choice of words.)

It was a fools' paradise. Virtually anyone with a subpar FICO score, including many real estate licensees, were led to believe buying any home would lead to easy fortunes being made.

Many buyers hoped that the increase in home values would bail them out before they were hit with increased payments. They often expected to resell, and many did, before the payments turned them upside down. In the ensuing mortgage meltdown, many bankruptcies occurred, with buyers turning their properties back to the presumed lenders.

Their fantasies worked for a while, then reality caught up when the bubble burst. The mortgage situation went downhill in a hurry. A great many mortgage lenders filed for bankruptcy themselves and fled the scene.

Many investors who had speculated on the continuing rise of prices and who had multiple homes they were purchasing with very little equity were suddenly upside down on their mortgages; they couldn't keep their properties rented and could no longer make payments.

A great many of those homes wound up on the auction block, with few buyers in sight. Prices plummeted sharply due to the glut of foreclosed homes on the market. Wall Street had sold a lot of mortgage-backed securities that were worth far less than their investors had paid for them. Wall Street rightfully bears a lot of blame for complicity in promoting the securities.

There are many bargain-priced homes on the market that most analysts believe may not have reached the bottom as of the date of this publication. The recovery in the housing market in general is not expected to be the horse race of the past. In the meantime, some areas are weathering the storm much better than others.

During the meltdown, the last buyer of a property bought primarily as an investment got caught in the inevitable collapse. Most of them bailed out in a hurry, and many were forced into filing for bankruptcy. Many lenders who were gleefully profiting from easy-to-get loans bit the dust also. Many bankruptcies in the lending industry followed the bankruptcies of the buyers of the homes. Many banks were also caught in the mess that followed.

There are areas in which prices are holding firm while next door prices are subject to further decline. If you are in the market to purchase a home, this may be the time to do so. But, be careful. Don't fall into a speculative role unless you are experienced and know what you are doing.

On the positive side, the naturally inherent drive to own your own piece of real estate is universal. The increasing populations will continue to be a driving force for buyers competing for that piece of land they can call their own.

Speculators are out there in force every day looking for bargains. You may be competing with one of them if the home in which you are interested is particularly well priced. As a potential homebuyer, you may be competing against speculators. Currently, there are lots of choices for the home seeker. That will not always be the situation. Presently, it's not imperative for the homebuyer to be that competitive. Looking for a good buy, not necessarily making a killing is sufficient motivation for many. If it does turn out that you have made a killing, so much the better. Population pressures will eventually cause prices to rise. It's inevitable.

CHAPTER NINE

Alternatives to Conventional Lending:

The Lease-Option

This is the most overlooked and potentially the best alternative to purchasing a home in any period of time, no matter what financial turmoil may be taking place. Even in times without economic stress, this may be one of your better choices for home ownership.

There are numerous reasons why this could be a great choice. In an uncertain market, perhaps the lease-options will suit your purposes better than an outright purchase, especially if your cash is limited, or you are trying to conserve your cash.

In general, these instruments are widely used by investors and by the general public that has become familiar with their use. They are a great tool for investing in real estate.

If the value of the property declines during your option period, you may be wise to renegotiate the price, or simply decline to exercise your option. You may forfeit your option payments in that case. It cannot affect your credit status, as would be the case with most defaulted mortgages.

If the value rises, you may stand to profit, sometimes handsomely. In many respects, it's like hedging your bets. The pros use them frequently.

Be sure to order a preliminary title report, however, before signing any lease-option. It the owner granting you the lease options loses his property rights due to foreclosure, your rights can be terminated as far as the option is concerned.

See a knowledgeable broker to consider this option if you are inexperienced.

1. Defining a Lease Option

A lease option is really two separate documents: (a) the lease agreement and (b) the option to buy agreement. These can be created as two separate instruments or combined into one document.

The lease portion is a typical lease contract, spelling out the terms of the agreement: when the lease becomes effective, for how long a period, when payments are due, penalties for late payments, the amount of the deposit, tenant responsibilities, etc. Obviously, the address of the property being leased must be disclosed.

The option portion should include a copy of a purchase agreement that becomes effective when and if the option is exercised. It will specify the amount of the deposit, what portion of the lease payments will be applied to the down payment or to the purchase price, if any, and other features of a typical purchase agreement. It will also specify where, when and to whom the notice of intent to exercise the option is to be delivered.

It may well be desirable to attach a copy of a title report to confirm the legal description and its title owner. It may also tell you if the owner is in default on his mortgage payments and possibly in danger of losing his equity. If that turns out to be the situation, you may be in prime position to bail him out or pick up the property very cheaply by cashing out his equity for peanuts.

These agreements usually are for the same term, starting with a beginning date and ending with a termination date. They do not necessarily have to be for the same periods of time, although most of them are written that way.

Lease options can be as varied as you want to make them. The term of the lease option will be specified. A three-year term is recommended as a minimum. However, that's not a hard and fast rule.

The option portion usually requires an additional deposit over and above that required by the lease. But this is also strictly negotiable.

When writing the agreement, be sure to create a lease for a 12-month period, with options to renew it annually. This will prevent eager-beaver lenders from construing the lease to be equivalent to a purchase. From your viewpoint, this is also desirable in the event you want to bail out of it early.

Prior to the time when the trust deed became the most common form of transferring title to a property in which a lender was involved, there was no valid reason for creating separate documents. With the advent of the trust deed, however, lenders could construe a lease option as a sale and could then force acceleration of the mortgage. And some lenders might not be adverse to that. Of course, they will tell you they are merely protecting their interests.

Today, lenders would be unlikely to do so, but it is better to play it safe. Therefore, we recommend creating separate documents: one for the lease and one for the option. You can record the option when you feel that you are getting close to exercising the option. It would also be wise to update the title report at that time. In fact, you may want to update it periodically.

2. The Pro's and Con's of a lease-option.

The lease option has all the benefits of owning the property without the expenses of making a large down payment, paying escrow fees and the cost of a conventional mortgage. In many respects, **this is ideal for many potential purchasers.** There are no artificial FICO scores required.

Traditionally, the parties would agree to a specified up-front payment for the option rights, which normally is far less than that required as a down payment by a lender. There is also a specified lease payment, which is usually made monthly; although that's not a hard and fast rule either.

Normally, the owner of the property agrees that a certain portion of the monthly lease payment shall be credited toward the down payment. This portion of the monthly payment continues to accrue toward the purchase price, should the option to purchase be exercised.

3. If you decide not to exercise your option:

All of those payments would, of course, be forfeited. The possibility that the optionor could not obtain financing when he or she approached the time limitations for exercising the option would be the only negative to the lease option. But then, perhaps you would have made a normal down payment on a purchase of a home under a standard purchase agreement, instead of being in the lease option. So, you would have stood to lose in either case. So, it's a bit of a trade off—one in which you may be better off under the lease option.

Of course, any improvements made to the property while under the option would also be forfeited, should the option not be exercised.

If you foresee any such problems with financing your option to purchase, it may be time to begin renegotiating an extension of the lease option with the owner. Rarely does a prudent individual who obtains the lease option have difficulty in exercising the option. If you can look far enough ahead, you may want to think about selling the property or selling your rights to buy the property. **(Yes, you can certainly do that!)**

4. Selling the property while under a contract for a lease option.

The advantages of the lease option exceed this slight negative described above. If the lease option were properly written, as we would suggest, the optionee could in fact sell the property to another buyer, if done so prior to the expiration of the option period.

All the optionor would have to do is deliver notice to the seller *(optionee)* that he or she is assigning his or her right to exercise the purchase of the property, along with a copy of the sales agreement that is being placed in escrow with the notice of intent to exercise of the option.

A copy of the purchase agreement would also be placed in escrow the same day, to secure the new purchaser's interests. You are merely assigning the right to exercise the option in this instance. Be sure to include the clause: "and/or assigns" where you note the name of the optionor in the initial option agreement.

One could also do an actual exercise of the option and then turn around and immediately sell the property to another buyer. Our suggested method noted above, however, avoids this unnecessary intermediate step in the transaction. It also has the advantage of being far less expensive by avoiding double closing fees.

5. More Advantages of the lease option:

The lease option is an excellent choice for those wanting a home but who fall short of cash for the down payment, or who lack the means of clearing up credit problems prior to buying a home. Even investors make use of the lease option to secure properties they wish to either acquire for residential purposes or to hold for investment purposes—or merely turn it over immediately for a nice profit.

Often, the lease option works well for situations that will allow the optionee to take possession of the property while providing time to make repairs and improvements. Their goal is to make the improvement so that the property will qualify for conventional financing, and usually at a value considerably higher than their option purchase price.

This preserves the investor's capital to make the improvements, and thus being able to cash out with a profit before the option period expires.

Such investors usually don't intend to live, at least for a long period of time, in the property. They usually want time to live there while making the improvements. (It's nice not to have to drive to the office in the morning since you may be working where you live, if you do this often enough to be considered a "regular"). They then sell the property and move on to their next project. Some investors have made an excellent living, or at least supplementing their income by following this procedure.

6. These days the number of homes on the market makes the Lease option attractive to many sellers.

There are many more homes on the market today in which owners are willing to look at a lease option, even if they end up leasing it for less than their current mortgage payments.

However, be careful if you are tempted to try a lease option if the current owner is teetering on the edge financially. The property could get repossessed while you are making improvements.

You can file your lease option agreement with the recorder's office, but that won't solve all potential problems. It would protect your lease rights but not the right to purchase the property since the lender's rights trump your rights to purchase under your option.

On the other hand, you may find yourself in a position to immediately exercise your option before a foreclosure takes place, and perhaps persuade he lender to discount the balance owed on the property.

In these current times, lenders will not be eager to foreclose, allowing plenty of time to secure financing, should you choose to exercise your option. The danger of a lender foreclosing is more apparent if your seller has a very high equity. In those instances, there are wolves around the lender's camp ground who would eagerly pounce on a quick deal, with the lender to acquire the property. And don't let anyone kid you; the wolves are out there and some lenders are prone to cater to them!

7. Protect your Interests.

If the property owner asks for a credit report, you may be prudent to ask for one on the owner as well. His financial status is just as import to you as yours is to the owner. Protect your interests.

If necessary, you can probably wrap everything up within six months before the lender reaches the foreclosure stage. It's not likely the lender would do that in these times and these circumstances, as long as the mortgage is kept current. The lenders have enough properties on their hands. They don't need more.

8. One document or Two?

The safest procedure would be to create separate documents—one for the lease, which can be for a 12-month period but also renewable for successive 12-month periods and a separate document for the option.

Neither the lease nor the option has to be recorded to have validity. But we do recommend recording the lease. Be sure to order a preliminary title report before executing the agreement, however.

Be aware that if another purchaser contacts the owner and writes up a purchase agreement without your option being recorded, you could lose your option rights. Recording the document puts the public on notice regarding your option rights.

If the owner were foolish enough to make an agreement to sell the property to another buyer*, your option to purchase, if recorded, would take precedence in a court of law. *(Some unscrupulous owners have been known to have done this.)

9. This may be the right time for you to consider the Lease option.

If you are interested in the lease option program you should discuss it with your broker. However, not all brokers are experienced with the lease option. Many agents and sales firms are reluctant to become involved, as they may have to defer, in most cases, their commissions on the sales until the option is actually exercised. This may be years away.

Most agents are reluctant to postpone their commissions. They also risk the possibility that you may not exercise your option and they would then be without a commission.

Talk it over with your broker who has been assigned to provide his services to you. If he is reluctant to get involved in a lease option, *and that's his right to do so,* then contact the author.

The author has had many years of very successful experience with lease options. If you would like to consult with the author or would like to have a referral to a broker who will professionally prepare the forms for you at a reasonable cost, please scan the QR (Quick Reference) Code on the inside of the back cover. You will be contacted promptly.

Since we are not a licensed brokerage in any state other than California, we cannot charge a commission to the seller in the other states. That may leave you with other options that we can discuss with you, such as a referral to one of our associated brokers in your state, or to discuss other options you may have. No charge is ever made to our members for consultation. Legal advice, however, will not be provided under any circumstances. That doesn't mean we cannot discuss normal real estate functions with a broker's advice.

Hard Money Lenders

Hard Money lenders are described as those private lenders looking for a higher return on their investment. Being cautious about not exceeding their limits for maximum exposure risk will always be evident.

Such lenders will always be around, ready to loan money at a rate that will undoubtedly be higher than with conventional lenders. Minimal exposure is the key for the hard money lender.

If, for one reason or another, you have difficulty qualifying for a conventional loan, the hard money lenders offer alternatives. These lenders normally don't like to make loans for more than 55 percent to 60 percent of the value of the property that's their security.

In this possible aftermath of the mortgage meltdown era, they may be less than enthusiastic to loan even 55 percent of the value. And the borrower must have a good employment history with visible income.

Interest rates will usually run to the maximum allowable by law. The lenders are not interested in your personal needs or wants. They just want reasonable security in the property and to know the borrower has sufficient income to make the payments.

It may sound a bit heartless, but that's what "hard money" is all about. Don't expect a sympathetic ear when you apply for such a loan. Nevertheless, such lenders can and do play an important role in financing individuals who may not qualify for a conventional loan.

In those circumstances, hard-money lenders can be a good source of financing, especially for those willing to take a year or more to clean-up their credit problems. They can then reapply for a much better interest rate, with normal terms, from a conventional lender. Hard-money lenders expect the borrowers to follow this route.

CHAPTER TEN

Mortgage Insurance May be Required

If you are required to have mortgage insurance, choosing the right lender may be very important. With less than 20 percent to put down, you may be better off looking for a lease option. (See the previous chapter.)

You may need mortgage insurance with less than 20 percent down, and that may boost your monthly payments. This poses somewhat of a paradox. The buyers with the least capital, frequently also the least capable financially, end up getting hit the hardest for monthly payments, along with a potentially higher interest rate.

The mortgage insurance payments will continue in force until your total equity is at least 20 percent of the value of the property at the time of purchase.

Some lenders, including at least one well-known bank, were continuing to collect the mortgage insurance payments, although their borrower's equity in the property was substantially greater than the 20 percent at which time the insurance terminated. The insurer, in the meantime, had dropped the insurance premium completely. Some sleazy bankers were continuing to collect the premiums from their buyers, although they were no longer required.

Beware of the scams! Check your lender's practices regarding collection of mortgage insurance premiums after the policy has expired.

Mortgage insurance is intended to protect the lender for the difference between the purchaser's mortgage amount and the typical 80 percent LTV. For example, if you have a 90 percent LTV mortgage loan, the lender wants insurance for the difference between an 80 percent LTV and the 90 percent LTV on your loan. The mortgage insurance protects the lender for that 10 percent of the loan amount.

When you continue to make payments on your loan, the balance should eventually drop to 80 percent, or less, of the original purchase price. The insurer's regulations stipulate that when the mortgage balance drops below 80 percent of the original appraised value, mortgage insurance is no longer required. Your total mortgage payments should decrease by the amount of your monthly mortgage insurance premium.

In the particular instance cited above, a well known bank decided they liked that extra income, which was now 100 percent pure profit to the bank, at their borrower's expense.

They declined to notify their borrowers that they needn't continue making those additional payments for mortgage insurance, even though that policy on their borrower's loan had expired.

By all reasonable thinking, it would be unethical to continue to receive the insurance premiums that were no longer required on their loan. The bank in question, a well-known national bank, apparently thought otherwise and continued to collect the premiums, failing to notify their mortgage borrower that the premiums were no longer required.

In this instance, which involved a bank that was federally chartered and was licensed in the state of California, the Attorney General of the state notified the bank in question that their practices were unreasonable, if not unethical. When the bank refused to correct their procedures the attorney general took them to court. The court ruled against the bank.

In defiance of the ruling, the bank in question declined to abide by the findings of the court. The bank's state license was then revoked in California. Rather than comply, however, the bank simply declined to renew their state license, arguing that since they were a federally chartered bank they didn't need to comply with the state's requirements.

At last word, the bank is still making loans in California and very possibly still collecting unauthorized mortgage insurance premiums from its borrowers.

You might be well advised to check the history of your bank, and other lender if you are contemplating getting a mortgage loan in which mortgage insurance would be required. Obviously, that bank was not the only lender with ethics problems.

Always ask your loan officer, no matter where you go for your mortgage loan, what their policies are regarding mortgage insurance. The biggest problem in doing that is that many mortgage companies promptly sell the loans to investment firms or syndicated groups, resulting from Wall Street activities. In some cases, even the bank mentioned above was purchasing these loans and applying their own ethics.

In taking out any loan, you may never know who might end up owning the loan in question *(or the deed, for that matter.)*

But, if the bank in question merely has the servicing rights, as was the case with the bank in question, they are merely picking the borrower's pockets, in the instance noted above!

Be sure to ask what your servicing agency has done in this particular issue in the past. Some banks are known to be very arrogant. They think that their federal charter entitles them to follow their own rules and ignore ethics.

This was not the only national bank that has been playing such games with their mortgage customers. The well-known Bait and Switch game will always plague the lending industry, although recent legislation makes it more difficult for lenders to play such games.

CHAPTER ELEVEN

Commissions and Other Seller Obligations

The Commission

If the property is in the Multiple Listing Service (MLS), as most are, the seller usually pays that commission. The commission rates are not supposed to be uniform throughout the multiple listing service membership; however, they usually are.

Most of the listing firms seem to be of the same mind when it comes to establishing commission rates. Real estate listing services and the state and national associations of the agents do not establish or promote any particular fee to be charged to sellers. To do so would be in violation of federal law.

If the property is a FSBO (For Sale by Owner), the commission may or may not be paid by the seller. The buyer may have to pay his agent's commission if the seller won't agree to do so. Does the owner profit from this arrangement? Typically the answer would be a resounding "yes."

There have been many instances in which the FSBO property owners were totally ignorant of all the real estate forms required today. A buyer, unless knowledgeable, could be at risk with a FSBO.

When viewing properties, you should ask how long the property has been on the market. If a good deal longer than the average listing takes to sell in that area, you can reasonably assume that it's probably over-priced, or that it has other problems that should be investigated.

In the mortgage meltdown era, it takes, in many instances, over 12 months for the typical listing to be sold; sometimes much longer. Even then, it may have gone through several price changes, to become more aligned with the market.

Most listing agents will have comparable sales or listings in the area of the home in which you might be interested. You may want to drive by these "comps" in order to feel comfortable with the listed price of the property in question. Request a title company provide comparable sales in the area of a certain property.

Title companies will normally provide comparables free of charge, but it will be necessary for you to specify the time frames in which the sales occurred. Looking for comparisons sold more than six months ago may be too long a period for accurate price comparisons. Check the comparables carefully. Your real estate broker can certainly get them quickly for you.

You don't want to end up in a situation which everybody in the MLS (Multiple Listing Service) knew the property was overpriced, but that you had no knowledge that might be the case, especially if you were being shown the property by the listing agent. The old expression, "Caveat emptor" (buyer beware), applies.

Listing agents who tend to be a bit conservative in their estimates of market value generally don't get many listings. Exclusive listing agents and dual agency agents are competing for listings. Obviously, most sellers will go with the agent who butters them up and gives them the highest estimates. That's one of the best reasons we can suggest for dealing strictly with Exclusive Buyer's Agents.

Sellers Obligated to Disclose Pertinent Information

The question is, "What's pertinent?" Sellers are required to disclose all known information about the condition of the property that may be of material significance. Obviously, they cannot be expected to disclose information about conditions of which they are not aware at the time.

For instance, recent heavy rainfall may have caused land to become unstable in areas where that never was a problem in the past. We see instances of this in news casts today.

If you buy a property in that area and after closing the transaction the rains create problems, is that considered "pertinent?" One would think so. But how do you determine if the sellers were aware that there might be a problem if he or she has never experienced it?

Change the story slightly. Let's suppose the seller knew of a small slippage of the land on or near his property, which had occurred eight or more years before.

Is that pertinent? Yes. It would certainly be pertinent. The seller would be obligated to disclose the fact, if he knew about it.

But suppose the slippage had occurred five years prior to the seller having acquired the property and that he was totally unaware of any problem.

Is that information now pertinent?

Yes, of course it is.

But the key is: was the seller aware of it? Whether he was or wasn't may be difficult to prove.

The buyer's best defensive posture may be, "don't take everything the seller or the seller's agent tells you as the gospel truth." Rely on the opinions of those of experts.

Don't make an offer to purchase any suspect property without your having a clause that allows you or experts you hire to make full inspections. In some instances the inspections should be at the seller's expense. In other instances, it may be the buyer who should pay. The advice of an Exclusive Buyers Agent is your best defensive posture.

Remember, however, **real estate agents are ethically bound not to disclose any privileged information** which may be adverse to their seller's interests, such as the reason for selling, or what the seller's bottom line may be.

Any information so disclosed that results in the seller getting less for the property than the seller has been advised by the listing agent that his propterty is worth is adverse to the seller's interests. You shouldn't expect an agent who represents the seller to betray that confidence.

Exclusive Buyer's Agents, on the other hand, have no such obligation to the seller. The real estate broker who will be representing you in any purchase transaction, if you are following the suggestions in this book, will acting as your Exclusive Buyers Representative.

He isn't concerned with getting the seller a good deal. He or she is intent in your getting the best deal he or she can possibly negotiate on your behalf. He isn't about to cover up any flaws in the property that he might discover. He will obtain the best information available as to the seller's reasons for selling.

FSBO's (For Sale by Owner)

If you see a home that has a For Sale by Owner sign, the so-called FSBO, be forewarned that some owners frequently try selling their own property because it may be overpriced. They may, in fact, have been told so by real estate agents they may have talked with.

The seller often has his or her own idea of what his or her property is worth, usually "hearsay," and will not be budged from that figure come hell or high water. They seldom go to the trouble of examining sufficient comparable properties to establish a fair market value for their property.

A number of For Sale by Owner, or similar such real estate companies, have sprung up across the country in past years, at least those years in which prices were continuing their upward spiral.

They usually work off a sliding scale of fees, anywhere from as little as 1 percent or a flat fee of perhaps $495, for example, to put the property on a list handed out to the public, should they come by. In the final analysis, it will likely be the seller who benefits from such arrangement, not the buyer.

Never get emotionally involved in any such purchase, difficult as that may be. There is always another property around the corner. Be willing to defer decisions until you have had a chance to sleep on it and to allow for consultation with an experienced person of your choice.

Let the experts handle the negotiations. An Exclusive Buyer's Broker is unlikely to blow the deal. Tact is the essence of successful negotiations.

By analogy, we can compare this situation to that of an attorney who represents himself in court. The well-known expression, that "An attorney who represents himself has a fool for a client." can apply equally to buyers.

Keep in mind when looking at properties that many people move every five to seven years. Even if you don't plan to move that often, keep an eye on features of the properties you see that may be appealing to all buyers.

Once in a home, you will undoubtedly sell it sooner or later, usually much sooner than later. Unusual properties that have limited appeal may be difficult to resell. Look for those features most likely to appeal to a majority of purchasers.

Location is Every Thing

Be concerned about properties adjacent to commercial or multifamily residential areas; avoid areas that are mixed—i.e. a combination of residential and commercial, or mixed single-family/multifamily areas. Values may not show as much appreciation as homes in residential areas.

If appreciation occurs, it will usually be less rapidly than well-defined neighborhoods with good schools and in preferred locations.

Homes on thorough-fares, or on other busy streets are generally less desirable and less salable than homes away from traffic. Homes in well-defined subdivisions with winding streets have more appeal than homes in older rectangular-grid subdivisions.

Look for obsolescent features in the house, such as outdated bathrooms and kitchens, or wiring that has not been brought up to code. **Inspect chimneys and fireplaces carefully**. Inquire as to whether hazard insurance can be obtained at a reasonable price for an older home with a fireplace that hasn't been updated.

Many insurers balk at insuring such structures unless the fireplace and chimney have been modified to meet current building codes. That could be expensive. Be sure to stipulate in any offer that the seller is responsible for such inspections and modifications, if necessary. Sellers may balk at this suggestion, but that's still your best option.

Inquire whether there ever been an incident of mold in the house that required extensive cleanup. Insurers have been burned on properties with this problem and will no longer offer insurance protection against mold or water damage, either of which is the result of owner negligence.

If you have any reason to suspect there may be a mold problem, have the home inspected, preferably at the seller's expense, to be certain you aren't getting into a serious problem that will then be at your expense to clean up later.

The three most important factors, according to most real estate agents, about any real estate investment are: location, location and location.

This has often been modified: *See an exclusive buyer's agent!* Now that's smart advice!

Chapter Twelve

Finding the Property that's Right for You

Be prepared to look at comparable sales in the area of the home (normally within a six to twelve-block radius for residential property within an urban area) for the past three to six months. Any title company can easily provide you with these. Title companies normally do not charge for them.

We suggest selecting three months, then expanding that if your title company has difficulty locating sufficient sales in your designated area. Here is a list of important factors you should take a careful look at:

(1) **The Neighborhood.** Look the neighborhood over closely. Is it the kind of area in which you feel your children would be safe in walking to and from school?

Would you feel safe strolling around the neighborhood in afternoons or early evenings? Talk to some of the neighbors and learn what they have to say about the area in which they live. Ask the neighbors if they would be likely to sell and move if they were to get a good offer. A high number responding "yes" will certainly give you a clue worth heeding.

Real Estate agents are forbidden by law from providing you with information about the characteristics of the neighborhood concerning race or nationality. For instance, if you ask your agent for such information, he or she must not provide that information to you. You must determine those factors without his or her participation.

(2) **Take a tour of the neighborhood,** both during the day and in the evenings and weekends. Be certain are no suspicious activities going on in the streets, no gathering of gangs. High numbers of individuals with tattoos could be a symptom of an element you may want to avoid. Even small children wandering the alleys and streets unattended can be a warning that the neighborhood may have problems.

(3) **College and universities districts:** If close to a college or university you may find your weekends disturbed with a continuous round of loud parties at all hours of the day and night. Look for signs of litter, such as beer and soda cans, strewn about the parking strip. It isn't likely to improve should you move into the neighborhood.

(4) **Schools**: Visit the schools your children will be attending. The quality of the schools is of utmost importance if you plan to raise your family there.

(5) **Police Department Records:** Check with the police department and determine how frequent are the calls of reported break-ins or gang-related activities in that neighborhood. What appears to be a peaceful neighborhood during the day could be a different story at night.

(6) **Street Traffic:** Listen and observe the street traffic. If there is a preponderance of shoddy-looking vehicles parked on the street or in driveways, to the extent that they give the neighborhood a negative impact, you may want to look for a home in another neighborhood.

(7) **Check the comps.** Be sure to review comps for size of the house (i.e. square footage), number of bedrooms and bathrooms, the number of garages and other amenities, along with the ages of the houses. Consider the location of each "comp" carefully. It would be wise to visit each to see that they are in similar areas and of similar construction.

(8) **Overbuilt homes in the neighborhood:** Avoid buying a house that is overbuilt for the neighborhood. Overbuilt means any addition to an average home in an average neighborhood that makes it stand out as a much larger home than the others in the neighborhood.

(9) **The best buy?** The best buy in any neighborhood may be that slightly run-down house that's priced below the others in the block. It is possibly one that everybody else is passing up.

That may be a sure signal the owner is in trouble with his mortgage and that he might be willing to sacrifice his equity for a pittance of its value. Be sure that you have the wherewithal to take advantage of that opportunity.

Do You Really Want a Swimming Pool?

Nearly all first-time home buyer seems to want a pool, especially if they have children. As a general rule, a pool does not add much value, if any, to a home when it comes time to sell.

Thirty-five percent or less of the new-installation cost would be a generous figure to use in determining the value the pool adds to the property, and then only if it's in excellent condition. If old and in poor condition, the value of the property should be lowered to accommodate removing or replacing the pool.

If the property you are considering has a pool, don't offer anything extra for it, unless it is of very recent construction, or in very good condition, and even then don't offer much.

If the pool is in poor condition, such as cracked concrete, broken tiles, etc., absolutely no value should be added. In fact, the price of the property should be lowered because of the expense involved in either removing or repairing the pool.

New pools can be very expensive to add to an existing property, should you consider doing so. They are unlikely to return in equity the amount you put into them.

Be aware that maintenance costs can be high, especially if you hire a pool service firm. Children often clamor for a pool, but when it comes to keeping up a pool, they are frequently nowhere to be found. On the other hand, the appeal of a pool to some families is undeniable.

Properties with pools are somewhat like boats; it is said that the two happiest days in the life of those who own them are the day they were acquired and the day they sold them.

Are you Obligated to Call the Listing Agent ?

Rarely. Most real estate firms are members of the local MLS. That means that any agent who is a member of the local MLS, or statewide MLS association, can show you the property. It isn't necessary or even desirable that you see the particular agent who has listed the property.

All members of the association are bound by the same rules. You will get the same attention with respect to any listing in that MLS regardless of which office handles the sale. Or, at least that's the way the MLS is supposed to work. Does it always work that way? Not all the time. For example, perhaps the listing agent has an imminent potential buyer in the process of making an offer to the listing agent, but the buyer is perhaps out of town on a business trip and will be back soon.

And who is going to blame that agent if he or she delays presenting your offer in order to present this or her offer when their buyer arrives back in town? And having viewed your offer he or she will know exactly what to tell his or her buyer in order to top it.

Is that ethical? No.

Does is happen? Yes, all too often.

Contingencies

Make your offer subject to satisfactory inspections and other investigations you may want to make. These are called "contingencies." The offer is called a "contingent offer."

Structure your offer so that it is contingent upon a satisfactory report from licensed contractors or an experienced home inspector. They will look the home over carefully for you and provide you with a written report.

Your Exclusive Buyer's Agent will have no problem taking this approach. If you are viewing the property with the listing agent, he or she may try to discourage any contingencies you want to include in your offer.

If something is overlooked that turns out to be a problem later, you will have someone else (the inspection company) to go after besides the seller and/or his agent's company.

Generally, contractors and Home Inspectors are insured. Be sure yours are licensed and well qualified. Ask for references. It's easier to get an insurance company to pay up rather than having to sue a seller, who may be long gone.

You may wish to hire more than one contractor, such as a roofing contractor, an electrical contractor or others. You want to assure yourself that you will have the highest comfort level with the property you may be buying. Discuss all such matters with your broker or his designated agent.

Be sure to get free estimates first, if possible. However spending a few hundred dollars for inspections may save you many headaches and considerable amounts of money later.

Renegotiating the Price May be Smart!

There's another advantage to having the home inspection done. Should anything turn up that might be construed as a negative, you can use that, perhaps, to renegotiate a better deal with the seller.

Maybe it's a minor flaw, perhaps a crack in the driveway pavement that can be repaired, but which could be quite expensive if you or the owner were to redo that segment of the driveway completely. You may not have given it much thought initially. But now it's beginning to stand out like a sore thumb.

Use this, for example, as a reason for negotiating the price down. Maybe it would cost the owner $5,000 to fully replace the concrete. So, why not get her to lower the price by $5,000.

Most likely, you would have no intention of repairing it, as it may well be of minor concern. Most driveways end up with cracks eventually. Unsightly? Yes, but most don't serve as a major deterrent, nor do they create a hazardous condition.

Be a fair but tough negotiator. It's your money. You can always threaten to walk away from the deal if the seller balks. Most sellers will yield and offer to make a concession in the price, perhaps compromising at half what you are asking for.

It's a rare seller who will walk away from a deal rather than make a concession, especially if they are already making plans to move or have other reasons why they want to sell quickly.

Often, the listing agent may offer to chip in for some of the costs. Go for it! Your Exclusive Buyers Broker can be of great help to you when it comes to negotiating or renegotiating seller concessions. After all, talk about incentives, your broker may be getting paid an additional commission for doing so.

CHAPTER THIRTEEN

The Financial Aspects of the Transaction:

(a) The Deposit:

How much of a deposit should you be expected to put up with an offer to purchase? This is sometimes referred to as a "good faith deposit" or "earnest money." Different parts of the country will use different terms, however, they all mean the same thing.

It is essential to include the deposit with your offer; otherwise the offer, if accepted, may not be binding on either the seller or the purchaser.

The deposit can be as little as one dollar. However, that would not impress either the agent or the seller as being a very sincere offer. From $500 to $1,000 with the deposit being increased to as much as 1 percent of the sales price on acceptance would usually be agreeable. Offers can also always be written so that the deposit can be increased in escrow after certain conditions are satisfied.

Some sellers think, mistakenly, they are more secure with a buyer who puts a large amount down as a deposit. There is no valid rationale for doing so, unless the buyer or seller is on an ego trip and wants to impress the other party. Since an experienced **Exclusive Buyer's Broker** representing the buyer can recommend all sorts of contingencies in the offer, the amount of a reasonable deposit should be of no great concern to the seller or the listing agent.

A contingency written into the offer ensures the buyer that the contingency must be satisfied, or the offer is null and void. If your agent advises against making contingent offers, it may be wise to get another agent, pronto.

You can always put an additional deposit into escrow when all contingencies have been removed, such as inspections, receipt of the seller's disclosure statement, examining the title report, etc. And it would not be unreasonable to do so.

In many cases **a Promissory Note in lieu of a cash deposit is acceptable.** Some agents may be totally confused if you offer such a note for the deposit, however. Most agents probably haven't been exposed to the use of notes if they have only dabbled in residential real estate—and then, only recently.

Promissory Notes can be a part of any real estate transaction. There is no valid reason for tying up your money when a substantial amount of your capital is involved, especially when contingent clauses could take several months to be removed.

51

In these days, "short sales" and foreclosures can take a long time to get approved, find a lender, and then to go through the normal escrow process. It would be foolish to tie up your money with a large deposit while such procedures are taking place. Notes can specify their being converted to cash when the transaction reaches the point at which the purchaser has no more contingencies remaining.

(b) The Closing Costs of the Sale:

In some areas, buyer and seller split the costs of title insurance and escrow fees, while in other areas the seller pays all costs, or the buyer pays it all. It generally reflects what is customary in the area in which the property is located.

No matter what may be customary in the area, it doesn't hurt to request that the seller pay for all the costs. All a seller can do is counter and offer to split them, or refuse—foolishly perhaps, if he's looking for what's customary in his area. Perhaps the seller is merely following his listing agent's suggestions regarding what is customary in the seller's area.

A shrewd purchaser, through his **Exclusive Buyer's Broker,** can play hard ball here, if desired, to extract some seller concessions on this issue. **It's your money!** Why should you be playing "Mr. Nice Guy" if you are intent upon saving as much of your money as possible?

It sometimes may come down to who is able to do the most bluffing, buyer or seller. If you are serious about buying a particular property, don't hesitate to do the bluffing.

If there are a lot of properties on the market in your chosen area, you can certainly play hard ball. If you are dealing with the listing agent as your representative, you can probably forget about getting any seller concessions.

(c) The Closing Costs of the Mortgage:

First-time buyers can be naive about what to expect by way of closing costs for the mortgage loan. Reading this book will take care of any possibilities of that happening.

Some buyers think that when the real estate agent tells them they and the seller will split the closing costs, it means the seller will also pay half the costs of the mortgage loan. The costs of the sale of the property and the costs of obtaining a mortgage on the property are totally separate items.

When we say that the buyer is fully responsible for the loan costs, it doesn't mean the buyer can't ask the seller to pay some of them. **A shrewd buyer or his Exclusive Buyer's Broker will do so,** in fact. Most lenders will allow the seller to pay some of the costs. The seller can contribute, usually, up to 6 percent of the sales price, toward your nonrecurring closing cost. *(Property taxes would be one example of a recurring cost. Title fees would be an example of a nonrecurring cost.)*

That's where smart negotiating comes in. He recommend including a clause that the seller pay the buyer's closing costs. Initially, your Exclusive Buyer's Broker would probably write your offer to have the seller pay all that are appropriate, or, at least, a good part of them. These contributions by the seller should be spelled out in the Offer to Purchase agreement.

This is no time to have a wimp for a real estate agent, especially one who may also represent the seller. Starting with 6 percent of the purchase price for a contribution to your closing costs may be a good point to begin your bargaining. Be sure the clause is stated clearly in the purchase agreement.

The seller may refuse. But so what? Make sure the seller's agent understands that you can walk away from the offer if the seller balks. The seller may end up offering to at least pay some of your costs. Take what you can get!

If your broker is being paid by his buyer to negotiate sizeable concessions, your broker will be very aggressive in making these proposals to the seller. Remember, your broker will negotiate with you as to what is classified as a "concession" that comes with a commission to your broker, or what concessions are not included in any commission agreement with the buyer.

It would all be spelled out in your Exclusive Buyers Broker agreement. Your broker will have reason to be much more aggressive in making offers if he stands to gain by doing so. That's why he's willing to share his sales commission with you. It's all to the buyer's benefit.

Chapter Fourteen

Factors to Consider Before Making Your Offer to Purchase:

A shrewd buyer will look seriously at the preliminary title report well before going to escrow to sign documents for any purchase, preferably well before even making the Offer to Purchase.

If there is anything in the title report that is the least bit questionable, the shrewd seller will have a preliminary title report in hand for his agent to show to prospective buyers. That way the seller will be aware of anything that might throw a monkey-wrench into his plans for selling.

Another strong reason for viewing the title report before making any offer lies in the fact that if there are potential title problems, such as a pending foreclosure, or a "lis pendens" (pending lawsuit), involving the property and its owner of record, this may give you some strong bargaining powers. Your Exclusive Buyer's Broker will surely recommend doing so.

Similarly, if there has been a recent divorce action, both parties may be anxious to dispose of the property. They will more than likely be willing to listen to offers, even if substantially less than the asking price.

Normally, listing agents are competing with other listing agents to promise the seller the highest value. They won't be looking for reasons to quote lower values.

Normally, the listing agent will not tell you of these factors. That would be adverse to his seller's interests. Listing agents are obligated not to voluntarily tell potential buyers of incentives for their making a lower offer.

More than one transaction has fallen apart due to certain items appearing in the preliminary title report. They may affect the buyer's decision to perhaps proceed toward making an offer to purchase the property. Your **Exclusive Buyers Broker** is your best insurance in protecting the buyer's interests.

Reviewing the Title Report

All standard real estate purchase agreements contain a clause wherein the buyer has a certain number of days in which to review the title report and to make known any objections thereto.

In other words, once having an accepted offer in hand, the buyer still has an option to not proceed should the preliminary title report show any negative factors that would cloud his intent to proceed with the purchase offer.

The purchaser in any purchase offer must disclose the factors in order to withdraw his offer without there being a potential for damages being claimed by the seller. Both buyer and seller would be smart to review the preliminary title report; in the sellers case, before putting the property on the market; in the prospective purchasers case, before making an offer.

Buyers should take pains to review the title report promptly. Don't wait until you show up in escrow to sign documents before having read the preliminary title report. Ask your broker or the title officer about anything in the title report with which you do not understand or agree.

If the closing is in an attorney's office, be sure to ask the attorney for a complete analysis of the preliminary report, along with your request that the attorney identify any potential problems.

The escrow officer will usually have the buyer initial the pages of the preliminary report when appearing to execute (sign) documents, indicating that you have read and that you understand everything in the report. Speak up before signing anything if you have any questions or if you find anything that you don't understand!

Seven Critical Factors:

(1) **Do you have enough cash** for the down payment plus the closing costs and ample reserves? Know ahead of time what's expected of you by way of cash for the down, cash for closing costs and cash reserves required by the lender.

(2) **If you haven't been prequalified**, see a mortgage broker or your bank's loan officer before you make an offer. Any loan officer can quickly prequalify you for a mortgage and print out a list of options for mortgages you may want to consider. That does not mean that you are obligated to place your loan with that particular bank, or mortgage company.

The loan officer can also promptly print out an advance Good Faith Estimate of your closing costs. Remember, however, even though they are supposed to be accurate, these are just estimates until you actually apply for a loan, get an approval and, preferably, lock in your rate.

(3) **Have you thought out all your options?** How high are you willing to go if your offer is countered? Unless you are represented by an Exclusive Buyer's Broker, you should be careful about disclosing this figure to any agent prior to proceeding with your offer.

(4) **What will your response** be if the seller refuses to budge from his asking price, or refuses to accept some of your stipulations? Have your made a determination as to what your bottom line will be? Are you ready to walk away from the deal if your bottom-line offer is not accepted? Perhaps you should consider your alternatives carefully before proceeding with an offer.

(5) **Have you stipulated in your offer** that the seller pay some, if not all, of your closing costs? Most loan programs allow the seller to pay up to 6 percent of the sales price toward the borrower's nonrecurring closing costs. Some lenders will even allow recurring costs, such as taxes, hazard insurance, prepaid interest, etc., to be paid by the seller. In these times of many distressed sales, it doesn't hurt to ask for such options. Your Exclusive Buyer's Agent will clearly earn his commission in this phase of the offer to purchase.

It would be extremely useful to know how large an equity the seller has in his property. It may be futile to ask for concessions that the seller can't possibly afford. Your Exclusive Buyer's Broker will be alert to these potential concerns regarding your offer.

The seller may accept your offer as written; or at least counter with an offer to pay something less than the 6 percent you may be asking for. Remember, you have the bargaining power. Play these cards while you can!

(6) Ask that the selling price include all appliances, even though the agent tells you they aren't included. Few sellers will pass up a deal over a refrigerator, a kitchen range or washer and dryer.

Even if you intended to replace them, they can always be sold for as much as several hundred dollars. If they are old, politely turn them down. You can save yourself the expense of hauling them to the recycle center, or advertising them as free to whomever comes for them.

(7) Buying a new home from a builder? Don't hesitate to make a low-ball offer with as many concessions as you would like the seller to grant. Builders need to move their houses. They can't afford to sit on them.

You may be able to save thousands of dollars. It happens every day. And this isn't something that an Exclusive Buyer's Agent is likely to overlook. Your conventional agent may not want to risk rocking the boat by including the items you are requesting in your offer.

Take whatever you can get. 1 percent on a $200,000.00 purchase saves you $2,000. Few sellers will quibble over $2,000 and risk losing a sale. Six percent can save you $12,000! How long would it take you to save that kind of money?

Ask for as much as your Exclusive Buyer's Representative thinks you have a good chance to get.

If you are looking at new homes, the builder wants to sell his homes. He has bills to pay, too. Don't hesitate to come in with a low offer. You may be surprised at what he will take. Builders normally have room for price cuts or adding extra features, such as an upgrade to carpeting, outdoor lighting, landscaping and other amenities.

Don't pass up the opportunity to ask for these extras. Most of the time, you will get them; or at least you will get some of what you ask for.

Most selling agents will try to convince you that the property is a good buy and won't last long on the market. Don't fall for that line! This is a common ploy by listing and dual agents. If you are dealing with an agent other than an exclusive buyers representative, insist on adding a clause to any offer you may make that states the agreement to purchase is subject to review by your attorney or by an independent real estate consultant.

Most real estate agents will usually blanch at this suggestion. They know very well that many deals are squelched, and often rightly so, because the buyer is seeking competent advice.

Take time to be sure all the financial details and contingencies are spelled out in the purchase agreement. Read all the pages of the offer carefully. If there is any clause you don't fully understand, request assistance from a competent advisor.

Consider These Check Boxes Carefully:

Usually, this is common on forms that reflect usage over broad areas that "customarily" do things differently than may be done in other areas.

Consequently, you will find a number of check boxes in the typical Purchase Agreement that may seem innocuous if you don't know the consequences of a simple check mark along with your initials. Some of them may mean that the seller pays for certain inspections, repairs and deficiencies resulting from a pest report. Check them in the wrong place, and you may end up paying for them.

As a simple rule, specify in your initial offer that the seller pay for everything that gives you an option. The seller can always make a counter offer, and very probably will, if he or his agent disagrees with any of your stipulations. Remember, the bargaining power lies in your hands. An exclusive buyer's agent won't leave you guessing at the full meaning of any clause in the purchase agreement.

Choosing an agent who also represents the seller may be a huge mistake. Yet, that's what you may be doing when you let yourself be represented by an agent who is not an exclusive buyers' agent.

Be sure the seller is responsible for the following:

(1) Replacing any broken windows and torn screens prior to close of escrow. Countless buyers have taken possession of the property they were purchasing only to find broken windows that were fine when the inspection was made a number of days earlier.

(2) Cleaning up the property before receiving the proceeds from the sale. Most agreements provide for a specific time in which you are entitled to reinspect the property prior to agreeing that escrow can close. Everything should have been completed by the seller before then.

Don't allow the transaction to be closed until the seller has met his obligations. Verbal agreements that may have been made are not binding. When a seller has received his money, you can kiss those oral agreements goodbye. It's unlikely the seller's agent will accept responsibility for things left undone.

For your protection, request that the seller provide a Home Owners Warranty. This will protect you somewhat from certain malfunctions of appliances, electrical, roofing and plumbing problems that may occur after closing.

It's a simple procedure to stipulate that escrow cannot be closed prior to your making a final inspection. The best time to check may be the morning before the transaction is due to close. Your broker can assist you in the process.

CHAPTER FIFTEEN

Your Loan Costs and Origination Terms

(1) Points:

This is a standard term used by lenders to denote the commissions on any loan they will be making to the borrower.

Your mortgage broker, or loan officer, represents the firm that is called the "Originator." They will provide you with an option to pay more points to get a lower interest rate, usually with higher overall costs, or fewer points to go with a higher interest rate, and possibly lower closing costs.

A point is 1 percent of the loan amount. A typical fee by most **Loan Originators** would be 1.5 to 2.0 points on an average $175,000 to $250,000 loan amount. Higher loan amounts should carry proportionately fewer points.

These fees are always negotiable between you and the **Originator**. However, don't assume that the point scale shown here will always hold for every loan. Smaller loans, usually under $175,000, for example, generally carry more points. Up to three points on a loan around $100,000 would be reasonable. The points quoted here are for well-qualified borrowers.

The typical originator generally needs to earn a minimal fee of at least $2,000 to $3,000 on any loan, regardless of how many points to which that equates.

The work involved in a smaller loan is every bit as involved as a loan of a higher figure. In fact, a small loan for a difficult borrower with credit problems may take much more work than a loan for a higher amount, but with a borrower for whom there is smooth sailing.

The tougher the work to get that loan for you, the more you should expect to pay. Check the GFE *(Good Faith Estimate)* provided by the originator and ask to have the fees explained to you. The fee being charged by the mortgage broker or bank will be clearly stated. If it isn't, start asking questions of your loan officer.

Remember, the points are always negotiable. Any lender who tells you otherwise is not telling you the truth. What he may mean is that he doesn't have the authority to negotiate with you. You can always tell the loan officer you will consider taking your loan elsewhere if they don't want to negotiate the fees with you. However, you also must be reasonable.

(2) Your bargaining power usually hinges on the quality of the loan you bring to the table.

The tougher the work to get you that loan, the more you should expect to pay.

Check the GFE (Good Faith Estimate) provided by the Originator; ask to have the fees explained to you. The fee being charged by the mortgage broker or bank will be clearly stated. If it isn't, start asking questions of your loan officer.

Remember, the points are always negotiable. Any lender who tells you otherwise is not telling you the truth. What he may mean is that he doesn't have the authority to negotiate with you.

You can always tell the loan officer you will consider taking your loan elsewhere if they don't want to negotiate these fees with you.

If you persist, your loan officer may hurriedly get up to go talk to his boss. They may think you're bluffing, especially if your lending institution is a bank. Most people tend to be a bit in awe of their bank and wouldn't think of challenging them. It's your right to challenge them any time that your money is at stake!

In addition to a processing fee of perhaps $400 to $699, the points are usually the only commission received by the originator from the borrower.

If there are other fees you don't understand or haven't agreed to, start asking questions. If they won't discuss their fees with you, don't hesitate to let them know that you can take your loan elsewhere.

In fact, you should shop your loan to see which bank or other lender will give you the lowest fees. Be aware, however, some lenders, including some banks, are prone to play the bait and switch game with their borrowers. They may promise a low fee to get you to apply with them, and then, when it's almost too late to take your loan elsewhere, they will lower the boom; they either charge you a higher rate or more points, and sometimes both. That's known as "Bait and Switch."

That's why banks may charge you a reduced fee for the appraisal so that they don't have to give you a copy. If you go to another lender, that lender has to order another appraisal, and by then you have already paid the bank for the appraisal, even if it was less than the fee charged to the bank by the appraiser. And don't think you will get any sympathy from the appraisal firm. They know which side of the bread their butter is on.

Before you settle on a lender, be sure to ask you broker for his advice. In many instances your brokers have had experience in the mortgage business. *The author has had a good many years experience in both the mortgage and the real estate business.*

The Wholesale Lender

The mortgage system can perhaps be compared to retail supermarkets vs. smaller neighborhood grocery stores. We all know that none of them grow their own produce. They all buy from distributors who buy from larger wholesalers. There is a great web of participating growers and marketers everywhere, all of whom are getting a piece of the pie.

The mortgage market is very similar in practice. There are "mom and pop" mortgage brokers, local community state-chartered banks, and credit unions. On the next level, you may find larger mortgage firms including national banks.

Above that level we find wholesale lenders that market their loan funding capabilities to the smaller mortgage companies. You may also have large national banks operating much like the large supermarket chains, but not necessarily giving their borrowers any better pricing for their goods.

These banks will often market their services to the smaller mortgage companies, acting pretty much as does a wholesale lender. Wholesalers often don't grow their own produce. They buy and sell to and from larger distributors.

In the mortgage look-alike market, Wall Street players may be the big movers in syndicating large amounts of loans to large markets, such as retirement and pension plans, large insurance companies and other large conglomerates.

Only one thing is certain—sooner or later your mortgage is apt to be marketed to one of the latter groups; or large syndicate groups on Wall Street will be packaging large amounts of mortgages to buyers all over the world

National banks and other groups in these circumstances usually keep the servicing rights to the mortgages while Wall Street is selling the actual mortgages in their syndications. This means that your bank may still collect your mortgage payments, for a fee, of course, and pretend they still own your mortgage. They have probably sold your loan, however, through the syndication process on Wall Street. In essence, they may pretend that they own your loan, whereas, in many instances they have merely retained the servicing rights.

Wall Street Always Gets Into the Game

When Wall Street gets into the game the syndicating game gets underway. Large numbers of the loans were sold to investors everywhere, including those loans they knew were likely to go bad if the economy began faltering. And falter, it did!

Sometimes more than one investor would own a piece of a loan. In many instances, the syndicators failed to keep track of the deeds, or who owned what.

This has led to problems when mortgage loan borrowers started going belly-up in the mortgage meltdown crisis. It was sometimes exceedingly difficult to track down and to prove who the actual owners were of a particular mortgage security and of the deed to the property.

In some instances, tracking down who actually held the deed was difficult to ascertain. Some courts have held that if the theoretical owners, *i.e. the banks that were holding onto the servicing right,* couldn't produce the deeds, proving they did in fact have the deeds, even it on behalf of a lot of owners, they had no standing in the court where foreclosure proceedings were being held.

This resulted in decisions by some courts to award a deed to the mortgagor, the one who had originally purchased the property and had secured a loan on the property through a bank or other lending source.

This summary is a brief, condensed version of a very complex system. It can be far more complicated than described here because of the layers of banks, mortgage firms, wholesale lenders, Wall Street, and the investment groups that are involved.

Wall Street's involvement often led to further complications. Multiple owners of the mortgages made it even more difficult to discover who owned what and where and could actually prove ownership of the deed.

Was there fraud involved in the syndication process? It became evident that some mortgages had been sold several times to more than one purchaser!

It may take a long time to sort everything out. Fragmented ownership of your mortgage can pose considerable problems to those claiming ownership of the deed. The banks that retained the servicing rights may act as though they are the owners of your mortgage, whereas the actual owners may be scattered throughout the world.

Service Release Premiums

Service Release Premiums (SRPs) are used by wholesale lenders as part of their normal pricing system of providing mortgage money to the retail markets. SRPs are akin to bonuses that the lender offers to their retail outlets. It is common practice for all wholesale mortgage companies.

This practice should have no affect on the mortgage rates your lender is providing to borrowers. Most SRPs are a fractional percentage, normally less than 3/8 of a point (3/8 of 1 percent) being quoted to the borrower by the lender. It's paid directly to the originator by the wholesale lender. It normally costs the borrower nothing.

However, the system of bonuses to retail lenders can result in abuses. Sometimes it is tempting for a mortgage loan officer to quote a slightly higher interest rate to a borrower in order to increase the SRPs his company would receive, sometimes by a full point or more.

These SRPs were previously not normally disclosed to the borrower. That practice has now been corrected so that lenders must make full disclosure to borrowers. That may decrease the temptation by some retail lenders, including banks, to pad their income from these loans.

For your protection, always stipulate that your loan officer or your lender must disclose to you how large the Service Release Premium (SRP) would be that your lender is getting from his wholesale lending source. If it's more than three fourths of a point, be sure to start renegotiating the rates being charged by your lender. Asking for a lower interest rate on your loan would be a good place to start.

Don't waiver on this issue! Protect your interests by stipulating that your lender must disclose all income they are making on your loan. By law, they are now required to disclose the SRPs that they are earning on your loan. If they refuse, tell them that you will take your loan to another lender. If you accounts are at that bank, you might also suggest you will take your accounts with you.

If your loan officer tells you, particularly if at a bank, that they had to charge you a higher interest rate on your loan, for whatever reason, start defending yourself.

Sometimes market conditions come into play, and for that reason it is wise to lock your quoted rate in early. However, immediately start asking your loan officer to tell you how many SRPs they are earning on your loan before you commit to their ordering an appraisal on the property. If it is excessive, over three fourths of a point, that should raise a red flag. They may be trying to take you to the cleaners, although that's not a given. Sometimes market forces or borrower decisions affect this process.

However, they are required to offer you the option of paying a higher interest rate and being charged a lower fee, or conversely, to secure a lower interest rate in exchange for paying higher fees. Have your loan officer spell it all out explicitly.

Don't for one minute think that because they may be a large national bank that they would never play the bait and switch game with you. Remember, mortgage loans are very profitable to the bank. Charging their borrowers a higher rate, even if a tiny fraction of a point, may be a red flag.

Shopping for a Mortgage Lender?

Unfortunately, there has never been an easy way to check the rates and fees your lender is proposing except to get quotes from a second or third lender. That's probably still the best route to follow for a borrower. However, be sure to do this within a single day; rates can change overnight, and it is not your lender's fault that it does.

The problem with this approach is that many lenders had been prone to quoting low rates and fees only so long as it took to get you to fill out an application. Once you did that, many lenders figured they had you hooked because of the time it would take to process your loan and gain approvals if you went elsewhere.

Large National Banks were prone to playing self-dealing tricks on their borrowers; they quote lower fees or no fees for your appraisal simply to prevent you from taking the appraisal to another lender. They may also refuse to give you a copy of the appraisal, claiming that since they paid for it they are not obligated to give you or another lender of your choice a copy of the appraisal.

They can, and normally will, refuse to assign the appraisal to another lender, even though you may have paid for it. Since the appraiser works for the bank, it doesn't help to ask the appraiser for a copy.

Our brokers are In the process of establishing a relationship with a national lender with whom we feel comfortable that we can ensure our buyers and members the best rates and fees available in the industry. Be sure to visit our website or discuss your needs with your broker and get his recommendations.

We do not recommend any of the lenders that advertise on national TV. Choose a lending source with representatives in your local community. Those who qualify will be able to look you in the eye. They live in your community and perhaps attend the same church you may attend. Their kids may go to the same schools with your kids. That certainly tells you something about their ethics. Such lender representatives can't afford "bad vibes" in their community.

ALERT! Don't sign any escrow closing documents on your loan until all fees have been clearly explained to you and that you have agreed to all the charges. Our brokers will be able to walk and talk you through the lending process. They will have the answers you may be looking for.

Your best defense is a sharp eye, while insisting on full disclosure of all fees being paid to the mortgage company or to the bank as part of your loan. They can voluntarily tell you how much they are making off your loan without breaking any laws.

Buying the Rate Down

The mortgage company, or your bank's mortgage division, is required to present you with options to pay fewer points to accompany a higher interest rate or more points to go with a lower interest rate. The latter is known as "buying the rate down. You will have the right to decide what you want to do.

It's a mistake to view loans solely upon the points being charged by your lender. It's important that you know which rate goes with what set of points. A zero point loan, for example, will surely carry a higher interest rate than one with a normal 1.5 to 2 points for the origination fee on a typical loan.

If you believe your mortgage company is charging excessive fees for your loan, be sure to request that they provide you with alternatives to paying those fees.

Do not hesitate to tell your lender that you want to get an estimate from another mortgage company before making a decision. Let your loan officer know that you are aware that many mortgage fees are negotiable. If they are unwilling to negotiate, don't hesitate to tell them you will consider taking you loan elsewhere.

That may not get you anywhere if you are visiting a banks' mortgage loan division. Their loan officers don't have much clout. Banks can be pretty stuffy and inflexible. Neither their federal charter nor their state license gives them the right to insult your intelligence.

You may want to go to an independent mortgage company, especially one in your own community. They have far more flexibility on your fees. Most are hurting for business, so now is the time to negotiate with them. Don't make the mistake of letting your bank, or any other lender, order an appraisal before agreeing to the fees they will charge you. That's the time to start negotiating.

If dealing with a national bank or a lender you haven't used before, one that you think you can trust, don't hesitate to let them know you are aware that some banks and some lenders have had questionable ethics in the past. Don't hesitate to let them know your have heard about lenders, including some banks, that were playing "bait and switch" tactics with their borrowers.

Choosing your Lender

Actually, few borrowers ever choose the ultimate lending sources for their loans. The typical borrower will have several choices for getting the initial funding for their mortgage, the most common of which are:

(1) A bank, usually licensed by the federal government and/or by the state, in the case of a community bank.
(2) A mortgage broker.
(3) A mortgage banker.
(4) A credit union.
(5) A direct lender who uses their own funds to initially fund the loan.
(6) A hard money lender who will make relatively short-term loans for a few years at much higher interest rates than conventional loans may carry.

The banks and some other lenders, known as mortgage bankers, may actually "close" the loan in their own name. But that doesn't mean they are not sending your loan on to the same wholesale lenders to which many other banks and mortgage companies send their loans.

How to Avoid Unscrupulous Lenders

The following are some critical questions you should ask your bank, or any other lender you may choose:

(1) Have you or your bank ever used bait and switch tactics with any of your borrowers?
(2) Have you or your bank ever declined to terminate mortgage insurance premiums when the borrower's loan balance had been reduced to less than 80 percent LTV of the initial loan?

(3) Have you or your bank ever received Service Release Premiums, or other such bonuses from wholesale lenders that were not disclosed to your borrowers?

If your bank or other lender refuses to respond, that should tell you something about their ethics.

It they tell you they have to submit the questions to their superiors at the bank or other institution, advise them that you will delay your application for a mortgage loan until they have responded to your questions.

If they get huffy with you, tell them you will take your mortgage loan elsewhere, and that you may take your bank accounts with you. The banks response to your questions may be an attempt at intimidation. No bank employee or executive has the right to do that. It will certainly tell you something about their ethics as well.

Look to our online newsletters for mortgage financing. We always look out for your best interests. If that means our making deals with lenders to pass on savings to our members, we will do so, and we will keep you posted.

Remember, there are no membership fees. Buying this book qualifies you as a member. Absolutely no obligations, ever! We keep you up to date via our online newsletters.

CHAPTER SIXTEEN

Purchase Offers Make References to these Features:

(1) Pest Reports

Pest reports may or may not be critical. Most purchasers would be well advised to insist upon them with any property built more than one year previously. Be sure your purchase agreement calls for one and that it be at the owner's expense.

Make sure that the report is subject to your approval thereon. Insist that the seller be held responsible for making all repairs called for in the report in order to receive a "clear" pest report clearance from the company that did the initial report.

Pest reports specify two areas of the property involved in the report:

(a) Those classified as Class 1, and
(b) Those classified as Class 2.

Those in class 1 usually require prompt attention. Class 2 involves recommendations by the firm making the inspection for long-term considerations. Class 1 is usually the one that lenders will require to be completed.

Some real estate agents may suggest not specifying that a pest report be required as part of the purchase agreement. Your real estate agent may suggest that the request for a pest report be placed in an addendum to the purchaser offer, which they will not submit to the lender. The lender, usually, will not require any clearance in that case.

This can be risky for any purchaser to approve of this division of the purchase agreement. Most lending firms are aware of such practices, but often overlook it, especially if the purchaser is putting 20 percent or more down on the purchase, or is otherwise considered a good security risk.

In order to avoid this hassle, most listing agents will instruct their sellers to secure a pest report when listing the property in order to face potential problems up front. This is the best course for them to follow.

Usually, the listing agent will advise the seller to agree to cover all costs of repairs up to a maximum of perhaps $1,000 to $2,500, if the report has not already been secured.

A prudent buyer will request that the report be paid by the seller and that all repairs required be at the seller's expense. An alternative would be to adjust the selling price downward sufficiently to cover repairs.

If the property is subject to a Short Sale or a foreclosure (the latter are referred to as an REO, i.e. Real Estate Owned by the bank or other lender in question.). The seller will usually be reluctant to cover any portion of the costs. In that event, it will be a judgment call on the part of the purchaser.

Your Exclusive Buyer's Broker can undoubtedly assist you in making these decisions, and possibly in getting the lenders to be cooperative with some of the costs. Buyers should be certain the offer to purchase states that their offer is subject to a written report being delivered to the buyer and to the buyer's satisfaction thereon.

If there are any surprises in the report, the buyer should reopen negotiations for price concessions if the seller is unwilling to pay the cost of repairs. Astute buyers can often drive concessions at this time. Your exclusive buyer's agent can handle these situations extremely well for you benefit.

(2) Appraisals

The appraisal may also note features that are obvious to the appraiser, such as dry rot in the eaves or cracks in the foundation. Most appraisers will protect themselves by stating that their report does not constitute a substitution for a pest report or a contractor's report.

However, both the pest report and the appraisal may serve as a basis for renegotiating price concessions if problems are noted that the seller is unwilling to correct.

Lenders will frequently call for second opinions by appraisal review firms, or even a second appraisal if they are at all concerned about values stated in the original appraisal.

Lenders will choose the appraiser and order the appraisals but require that the charges be paid by the purchaser prior to placing the appraisal request. Some real estate firms have been fronting the appraisal fee, which is to be repaid by the purchaser at closing. It can be risky for the broker to take this action. They often wind up eating these costs when lenders reject the mortgage applications.

The borrower never has a choice concerning the appraiser. This is strictly between the lender and their appraisers. The borrower does have a right to see the appraisal, as the borrower is paying for it. Many lenders will actually give them a copy of the appraisal, which is the right thing to do since the borrower is paying for it.

The exception may be in the case of the lender being a bank. Banks generally do not like borrowers taking matters into their own hands and possibly pulling the loan from the bank when better lending offers may be present.

The borrower should probably refuse the bank's request for the borrower to cover their appraisal costs if the bank will not provide a copy of the appraisal to the purchaser. Banks tend to refuse to release the report to the purchaser or to another lender even though the borrower has paid for it.

If your bank follows these tactics, they should not charge the buyer for the report. Banks may flout their intent by charging the borrower less than the cost of most appraisals. Usually, the banks have special contracts with the appraisers for reduced fees being charged. The bank doesn't want to make it easy for the borrower to take the loan elsewhere.

Sometimes a borrower will be requested to pay the appraiser by check at the time the appraiser arrives to do the appraisal. Wholesale lenders do not permit the report to be ordered directly by independent mortgage brokers.

(3) Escrow, Title, Taxes and Insurance Fees.

Escrow and title fees are usually non-negotiable items set by the title and/or escrow companies or by the attorney who may be involved. However, the buyer has the right to choose the escrow company and the attorney. It may pay to shop around and see who has the lowest fees.

The buyer receives a title policy insuring a clear title to the property. The lender receives a policy insuring the lender against defects in the title covering the amount of their loan. The borrower pays both premiums, and that may be fair.

A purchaser should always ask that the fee for insuring title be paid by the seller. This does not include the lender's portion, however. It never hurts to ask that the seller pay all of these costs. You would be surprised at how often they will do so.

Agents who represent the seller will usually resist the proposal. This is another good reason to choose an Exclusive Buyer's Representative and not an agent who also represents the seller.

Prepaid Taxes and Prepaid Hazard Insurance: The lender will normally require that 12—to 14-month's hazard insurance premiums be paid up front. Anywhere from four to eight months of real estate taxes are normally paid up front.

With down payments of less than 20 percent the lender will usually require impounds in which 1/12th of the annual insurance costs and 1/12th of the annual taxes be collected with each payment.

It the property is subject to homeowners association fees, the lender will usually add those fees to impounds required. The lender will then make your payments for taxes and insurance and homeowner's fees from your monthly payments.

Mortgage Insurance: If the down payment is less than 20 percent, lenders usually require mortgage insurance, which will result in an increase in your monthly payment. This area has been subject to impropriety by some lenders, notably banks.

Escrow Fees: The fees charged by the escrow company, or the attorney in those states or areas where attorneys close the transaction, are usually not negotiable. You can, however, check with other escrow and title companies, and with attorneys to see if they have lower fees. You have the right to shop for the lowest fees charged by title, escrow, and/or attorneys in those states where attorneys close the transactions.

Prepaid Interest: The lender will charge interest on your new loan from the date of closing to the end of that month. One full month will then elapse before your first payment will be due. Interest accrues during that month, and your first and subsequent payments will include principal and interest.

Bean in mind, you have an absolute right to negotiate any of these fees. You are not obligated to choose the title company the seller wants you to use. It's the buyer's choice, always.

Closing Date: If you are trying to conserve your cash, always try to get the closing scheduled early in the month. You would then be charged more in prepaid interest, however.

You will then also have a longer period (almost up to two months if closing is scheduled very early in the month) before your first payment falls due. That date would be on the first day of the second month following the month in which the transaction is closed. Since lenders have grace periods, usually 10 days to 15 days, you can gain extra time before making your first payment.

Other fees: There may be additional miscellaneous fees to cover recording, wiring of funds to the escrow company from the lender, overnight document shipping fees, and other miscellaneous charges. These have been referred to by numerous borrowers as "garbage fees."

Check with your loan officer for a more complete explanation of any fees you do not understand. Don't hesitate to ask your loan officer to cover miscellaneous fees.

CHAPTER SEVENTEEN

Another Alternative to Buying a Home

A Rent vs. Buy Analysis May Save you Money

Before you decide whether buying a home is the right course for you, consider getting a Rent vs. Buy Analysis to see if continuing to rent might be a smarter option for you, especially if you plan to be in the home for just a few years. Rents vs. Buy analyses are free. They can be found at a number of websites.

Your costs of an investment in a home, including mortgage initiation fees, can easily add as much as 5 percent to 8 percent to the original cost of the home. This may not include real estate taxes, upkeep, interest on the mortgage, mortgage insurance, homeowner's fees, and other costs.

At the other end, selling a home generally costs another 6 percent to 10 percent. That's a combined equivalent to adding 11 percent to 18 percent to your cost of the home—first buying it, then selling it. Subtracting alternative rental costs of 1 percent to 2 percent per year, your home would have to appreciate at the rate of approximately 2 percent to 3 percent per year for five years in order to break even—assuming there is no appreciation. And that doesn't include interest you might have been earning on you down payment funds!

Don't overlook repairs and maintenance cost on the home. We would expect that planning to stay in the home for at least five years should be considered. Of course, these are only estimates.

Obviously, other factors would have to enter the formula in order to be definitive. No allowances have been made for such features as swimming pool maintenance, landscaping and other such costs.

If short term is what you are contemplating, be sure you are either getting an exceptionally good buy on the property (*your purchase is well below market value*). Or appreciation will cover your costs in the next few years, which is unlikely given the current market.

Obviously, appreciation does play an important part of increasing home values. In some areas, homes will appreciate more rapidly in value than in other areas. Yes, currently prices in general are depressed. But historically that will change simply because the population will continue to increase. Buying in a depressed market is maybe smarter than waiting for prices to start increasing.

What Escrow is all About

Signing the Closing Documents
for your Purchase and/or your Mortgage Transaction

After having made your purchase offer and when all counter offers have been agreed to by each party, the transaction will move to the escrow phase.

In some states and in Southern California, attorneys may handle many of the escrow functions. In Northern California and other areas, escrow and title firms combine these separate facets of buying and closing the sale on any real estate property.

The process begins with your real estate agent, in most instances, delivering the original of the purchase agreement to an escrow company or an attorney. Your mortgage broker or lender will have a copy and will order the appraisal. Your lender may have already started processing your mortgage application. The appraisal will be ordered as soon as a copy of the executed purchase agreement has been delivered to his office.

Hopefully, you will have been preapproved for a mortgage. This will then be a relatively painless procedure and your transaction can proceed smoothly to the mortgage approval process and then to the closing phase. Your lender will deliver the funds to close the transaction when the escrow agency confirms that everything is ready for the final stage in the close of the transaction.

In some areas the closing functions are handled by attorneys. In virtually all of Northern California, attorneys seldom become involved. The escrow transaction, signing documents, etc, are all handled by an escrow officer.

The pro and con for using an attorney is that an escrow officer can interpret the title report. But she, or he, cannot give you legal advice. If you feel you need legal advice, see your attorney. In those escrow offices that use attorneys, the attorney will answer any questions you may have.

In most cases, however, a simple interpretation by the title officer may be more than adequate. Your Exclusive Buyers Broker is usually highly experienced and may be a good source of information. He, too, however, will not give you legal advice.

Be sure you have read the title report before arriving at escrow to sign documents. If you have any questions about any item noted in the title report, be sure you have had a full explanation by your title officer, or attorney. Do not wait until the last minute. Many transactions have fallen apart because the buyer failed to read the title report before going into the escrow, or attorney's, office to close the transaction.

It is recommended that the real estate listing firm order a preliminary title report well ahead of time, to lay to rest any potential title problems that may be present.

CHAPTER EIGHTEEN

The Mortgage Meltdown Era

In the wake of the mortgage meltdown era that began roughly in late 2006, the crisis has played havoc with the real estate and mortgage markets. Huge numbers of foreclosed homes have flooded the market. Obviously, this affects values.

A home that stands vacant is nearly always subject to vandalism. Lenders, if they are the true holders of the deed, may often lose their shirts on properties that have been vandalized. Therefore, in an attempt to lessen the likelihood of vandalism occurring, the lender will often attempt to leave the defaulted buyer in possession while proceeding with what is known as a "short sale."

A short sale simply means that the lender will suffer a loss—that's a foregone conclusion—but hopes that by leaving the defaulted borrower in possession, the risks of vandalism will be much less. It is called "short sale" because the sale price established by the lender is short of the remaining amount due on the mortgage.

The lender decides what his bottom line is as far as the mortgage is concerned, and then the property is listed with a real estate firm in order to sell it at a reduced price.

With a foreclosure, the former owner is evicted, and the house stands vacant. The lender knows there is a risk but assumes that the risk is probably the lesser of two evils. The lender wants the property sold and out of his hands.

If the former owner remains in the property as a tenant, a buyer wanting quick possession may be turned off by the presence of the former owner who is now the tenant. The lender knows that a tenant can be risky too. The tenant and former owner may badmouth the property in order to discourage buyers. They can then look forward to staying in the home for a longer period of time.

The other side of the coin? With short sales the lender may not be as generous with the discounted price as would be a lender sitting there with a vacant house on his hands.

In either case, the mortgage has usually been sold or syndicated to a group of investors, many of whom may likely be overseas. Lenders frequently have a difficult time tracking down the current holders of the deed. This has created problems in some instances, with lenders attempting to foreclose on properties for which the current claimants to the deed cannot produce the deed. Their claim to title is therefore clouded

Foreclosures can be very time consuming, as the lender has to track down the owners of the mortgage and relay any offer they may have to the group of investors to get approvals. In either event, it may be a difficult proposition for the owners of the defaulted mortgage.

Many of the banks that were collecting the mortgage payments were then left holding the bag with large numbers of homes requiring maintenance. The banks couldn't handle the task and let the properties deteriorate.

Population pressures just won't go away. The market will eventually come back.

Chapter Nineteen

An Invitation to our Readers:

Who couldn't use extra income these days? Generating some additional income without having to become a real estate agent can be a great way to go. Putting the knowledge you have gained from this program into a profit potential makes good sense.

We certainly recognize that it isn't for everybody, however. Simply treat it as an option you have. There are no contracts to sign, no warranties made of your being able to earn any income, and no obligations of any kind to continue if you choose to try this program.

Mentoring is the highest form of teaching. It's a natural for those who have benefited from the programs taught in this book. Become a mentor and discover some benefits from the knowledge you have gained. Of course, doing so is strictly optional, but why not? You can certainly see some financial benefits with very little effort. You do not participate in any commissions. You are simply paid a fee for the teaching process.

Become a mentor to your buddies and their friends. Teach them first how to order a copy of this book. And remember, it must be an original copy; no borrowed books will do.

Show them how to find properties they might be interested in purchasing and then show them how to follow the steps you may have taken to make a purchase of a home or other property under this program. Be ready to assist them in any of the processes found in this book. That's all you need to do.

That's what mentoring is all about. Show them how to get a copy of the book, hen assist them with the processes involved.

Mentors may receive a fixed fee for each home purchaser they help in the teaching process described in this book. They will follow exactly the same steps you have may have followed, if you have acquired real estate through this program.

The benefits are exactly the same for all participants. Become a mentor of one or more persons, do some training, and then perhaps put a bundle of money into your pocket just for doing some teaching. It's a win-win situation for everyone.

None of the funds for teaching comes at the expense of the home buyer. The company behind this publication has arranged for the funding of the teaching process.

If you are interested in becoming a mentor, the contact information go to the website: www.wegotclout.com.

CHAPTER TWENTY

The Author's Page

The author, self-described as an entrepreneurial real estate broker, has always been an innovator. This book promises a program for home buyers that takes the element of greed out of the picture. It guarantees smiles on the buyer's faces, and puts welcome savings into their pockets.

With a storied career in buying, selling, sometimes developing, islands in the Pacific Northwest and in Canadian waters, the author ventured further afield. Hawaii and the South Pacific group of islands, some no more than tiny dots on the map, beckoned; others, like New Zealand and the extraordinary Fijian islands, were to yield almost unbelievable adventures.

Clients ranged from a few celebrities and movers in our society to the less well-known, the Individualists, such as the retired airline pilot who just wanted to own his own island in the sun. *One of the author's real estate associates was a former Pan-Am pilot who sometimes piloted the company's single-engine Cessna in our closer-to-home-base property ventures.*

Some islands were quite handsomely priced, like the one we sold for one million dollars, all in cash, all US currency, along with a generous commission; others were, in today's terms, just a drop in the bucket. The author once sold a small seven-acre island in the Gulf Island group in British Columbia to a young woman whose father was a Washington, D.C. attorney. It was one of a cluster of small islands in which some of the well-established Seattle families for decades had their own private islands. A chartered seaplane originating in Seattle got us there quickly, after a short stop at Canadian customs. The tour didn't take long, even to the somewhat disheveled, vacant cabin. The island sold itself to a very happy client.

Upon taking an offer to her to resell it a few years later at a very considerable profit, her reply was, *"Thanks, Gil, but, no thanks! Every girl's got to have her own island!"* That's as classic a response as could ever have been imagined. It couldn't have been more aptly put, and no one has come up with a better response, in the author's opinion.

Most clients were looking for their own unique get-aways. They weren't necessarily well-known or even wealthy; many were just ordinary people with a spirit of adventure.

The South Pacific Islands ventures were usually exciting. Rarely did the author return without a new tale to relate. There are many the stories to tell; a forthcoming book, **The Island Buyers**, the authors next literary offering, may soon be completed.

However, even good things come to an end. A number of years later, wearying of long flights, living in hotels or sometimes funky cabins on the beach, often for extended periods of time, family and friends at home became of greater importance. On a visit to California a number of years later, the author was presented with some intriguing proposals. A former vice-president of a large Savings and Loan institution that had bitten the dust in the meltdown of the 80s persuaded the author into becoming a mortgage broker with his firm. It would be the start of a new adventure.

Some years later, with the retirement of his friend and owner of the mortgage company, the author and a close friend decided to focus on software, which was by then just beginning to become a factor in the mortgage industry. After some success, a graduate of the University of California in Chico, who had majored in computer technology, came to work as a programmer. Shortly thereafter, the programmer and his buddy, who had just graduate with a degree in business administration, hinted they would like to see the author open a real estate and mortgage company in Chico, California.

After some thoughts and some cajoling by the two buddies, the author agreed, particularly since the programming was a in a hit or miss cycle in those early years of computer technology. The expense of hiring programmers was going through the roof with potential payoffs well down the road. Each or the two buddies obtained their real estate licenses, and we formed Homelink Mortgage Corporation and Homelink Real Estate, one of the very first firms in the country to do both activities.

After doing some training, the business grew rapidly. We soon began hiring and training more agents. In the meantime the programming venture was draining the profits from the real estate and mortgage operations. That was the end of our software programming.

The real estate and mortgage companies continued to expand, including branch offices in Central and in Southern California. The agent initially hired as a programmer soon became a whiz in the real estate and mortgage field, while his interests in programming diminished rapidly.

Four branch offices and several years later, the roof began caving in. The new meltdown had hit. Real estate agents began dropping out like flies. Offices began slimming down dramatically, or closing entirely. It was a familiar story for many real estate and mortgage firms in the country. Lenders who had plunged into the subprime market, filed for bankruptcy. A lot of our lenders no longer existed. In the ensuing months with agent's having trouble making a living, the author had reason to reflect on the aftermath.

Was there something fundamentally wrong with the way the industry carried out its endeavors? Was it so bound up in tradition that it had trouble functioning in tough economic times?

Analyzing the problem, it became clear that larger big-name franchised real estate firms had their own theories about the real estate module that had become common: hire many agents, put them in little cubicles and give each of them some time on the floor for a couple hours per week. During that time, all calls were funneled to that particular agent. The system worked fine when times were good; Agents competed with each other. Those that weren't successful at meeting the managers goals were let go. Another agent filled the vacant tiny office. The system worked fine when times were normal.

With the meltdown, firms began losing agents. Some closed their doors entirely, others tightened their belts. The crisis had changed the face of the industry. Everyone was looking for answers.

The author thought about his own business model. What had led to his success, even in tougher times? Many of his clients had sought him out based on recommendations of their friends. Usually, the clients would come to him saying virtually the same thing, "I have already seen the property I want to buy. You don't need to bother showing me other properties. All you have to do is write up my offer. Would you consider making some concessions on your commission in my favor?"

Usually laughing, the author often replied, "So you have heard about me. How much of my commission would you consider fair?"

"Well, since your didn't have to find what I was looking for, and you don't have to chauffer me around the countryside looking at properties, how about a rebate of one third of the commission?"

Sometimes they would venture asking more of the commission, but they were always reasonable. They knew that our agents usually got a good chunk of the broker's commissions. If the broker didn't have to pay his agents anything, he would have money to spare.

All the broker had to do was review the property with his buyer, then write up the offer with the broker's suggestions on price, and possibly going after some seller concessions in favor of the buyer. It was, perhaps, another reason buyers came looking for "the broker who makes deals with his clients," My clients were no dummies. They knew how the system worked.

One thing most of my clients all seemed to have in common—they had an entrepreneurial spirit!

Brokers in smaller shops can easily handle all the business. Most of us hire agents who come looking for a place where they can hang their shingles, and rely on the broker to provide the opportunity to generate business. Most of the agents wanted to chase listings as well as represent buyers; they also preferred brokers who provide first-class offices, all at the expense of the broker, of course.

Usually, most agents meet their clients elsewhere. Agents were increasingly meeting clients at the local restaurant with our laptops under their arms. A small office with a small crew, and the tiger logo on the door, should work fine for most brokers and their agents.

The meltdown has been devastating. Virtually every facet, everything proposed in this book which was the result of the meltdown, has been tested in the author's own brokerage practices. This is a program that will work for those of us willing to learn how to better cater to their buyers. It's a concept that's easily embraced. Buyers everywhere will be delighted. There are enough benefits for everyone.

Message For Real Estate Brokers and Agents:

The economic crisis in which the country finds itself makes this an opportune time to present a new approach to an old industry. Keeping pace with the changes in our society involves an emphasis on innovation. Are you up to the challenge?

As the broker and CEO of **The Buyers Edge Real Estate Group**, I will be delighted to discuss contracts for agents. Brokers in California and other states are welcome to discuss opportunities, including some franchise like proposals, especially if they are looking at multiple offices.

All are more than welcome to inquire. There are some very sweet deals in our contracts for agents in California. But remember, you are responsible for you own expenses and office space. With internet capabilities any of us can work out of our homes, or we can join forces with other agents for office space.

What will we do for you? We will be marketing the book and the program extensively. We'll be happy to refer our readers and buyers to the agents and brokers under contract with our firm.

Commonly Used Terms in the Mortgage Industry

Amortization—The process of repaying a mortgage loan gradually, with equal periodic payments combining principal and interest. Your payments are calculated so that the debt is paid off in full by the end of a predetermined period of time, such as 30 years or 15 years.

Annual Percentage Rate (APR)—A measure of the total cost of your mortgage expressed as a yearly interest rate. The APR is usually higher than the advertised interest rate since it includes interest, points, and other finance charges. It is designed to help you compare and determine the relative cost of loans you are considering, but may be quite useless to most homeowners in making decisions since it does not include all costs of the loan. The calculation formula arbitrarily selects certain costs defined as Prepaid Finance Charges. This term is in itself confusing since lenders use similar terminology to define certain other costs that are prepaid, such as taxes. Taxes, for example, are a prepaid cost, but they are not a prepaid finance charge.

This may be confusing to most borrowers. Remember, it was designed by government experts. But take heart, very few loan officers or even escrow officers can provide you with a clear definition that can be easily understood. And don't try calling the Federal Reserve Bank; they may not know either. But they will cheerfully offer to "send you a pamphlet which will explain it all." Don't bother. You will be vastly disappointed and probably even more confused.

We suggest you ignore the APR as any real measure for comparison of loans. The only time it might be useful is if the APR is a great deal higher, meaning a full one-and-a-half points or more, than the note rate on your loan. Then, you should begin looking into your mortgage documents to see why it is so much higher and request a clear explanation from your loan officer or lender. Don't wait until your loan has closed!

What's more confusing is that two mortgage companies can be advertising the same loan with the same interest rate, but each may have a different APR since they may use different prepaid finance charges in their calculation, and both can be correct.

Appraisal—A professional estimate of the current market value of the property. The lender will generally use the lower of the purchase price or the appraised value to determine the loan amount.

Assessed Value—A value given to the home and property by the local assessor, which is used solely for determining property taxes. This may not be a good determination of market value.

Asset—Anything you own that has monetary value, including cars, household items, cash, stocks and bonds, and real estate. You are required to list your assets when applying for a loan.

Most often, the lender will require that some of these assets be verified. Examples of assets that are not usually verified for mortgage purposes are estimates of the worth of your home furnishings, artwork, jewelry, automobiles, etc.

Assets listed as bank accounts usually will be verified. If critical to the loan approval process, the value of stocks and bonds may also be verified.

Balloon Mortgage—Typically, a fixed rate mortgage amortized over a 15—or 30-year term, and which comes due with a lump sum (balloon) principal payment prior to the end of the term. For example, second mortgages frequently may be amortized over thirty years but with the balance owing at the end of 15 years to be paid in full at that time. That payment is termed a balloon payment

Biweekly mortgage—A mortgage based on a payment every two weeks. You would have a total of 26 payments per year, rather than 12 monthly payments. In effect, the borrower is making one extra monthly payment yearly. The loan, therefore, pays off earlier than a regular monthly payment schedule. This is one way for the borrower to save a good deal of interest on the loan.

Closing—After all negotiations on the price and other terms of the property have been accepted, the transaction enters an escrow phase. In some states, a meeting is set up with the buyer, seller, and lender (an attorney is often present). At this time, the buyer receives the mortgage loan amount needed to purchase the property and pledges the same as collateral or security for repayment of the debt. The mortgage documents are signed, and the title to the property passes from the seller to the buyer.

In a good many states, an escrow company handles the "closing" responsibilities. Attorneys are usually not present. Borrower and seller often do not appear at the same time to execute the documents. The lender forwards the documents to escrow for signing and the escrow officer conducts the signing session. Rarely does a representative of the lender appear at this time, although a conscientious loan officer will often accompany his borrower to the signing and will answer any questions by the borrower that may arise at that time.

Closing Costs—The fees that are entailed in any transaction involving property and a mortgage. These fees may be modest or they may be extensive. Some may be paid by the seller, but most are paid by the borrower if a mortgage loan is involved. Typically, the fees will equal about 3 to 6 percent of the purchase price and are all due and payable at closing, hence the term "closing costs."

Collateral—Property and/or other assets pledged as security to the lender (mortgagee) for repayment of your debt.

Conventional Loan—A term describing a mortgage loan made by an approved lender where the debt is not insured by a government agency such as the FHA or VA.

Convertible Mortgage—One version of an adjustable rate mortgage (ARM) that can be converted to a fixed-rate mortgage, providing certain criteria are met and the borrower feels it is advantageous to do so.

Discount Points—A one-time charge paid by the borrower, or by the seller if the seller is willing to do so, and which may be used by the lender to reduce the interest rate charged for the mortgage loan. One point is equal to 1 percent (1%) of the loan amount. On a $100,000 loan, 1 point would equal $1,000.

Escrow Account—The lender may have the borrower establish this account to set money aside which is earmarked to pay taxes and insurance on the property. A portion of every mortgage payment goes into the escrow account. The lender is responsible for paying the tax and insurance bills with these reserved funds. Also known as an impounds account.

Equity—The difference between the market value of the home and your remaining mortgage balance. As you pay down the mortgage balance, your equity or ownership in the home increases, at least theoretically if taking reduced valuations into account in times of recessions.

FNMA (Fannie Mae) and FHLMC (Freddie Mac)—These are two quasi-governmental institutions that purchase loans which meet certain strict guidelines. Having a guaranteed market for their loans makes it easy for lenders to turn over their capital quickly and to continue to make new loans. After selling the loans to Fannie Mae or Freddie Mac, the lender may continue to service the loan.

If there were no market for these loans, which may become securitized and held by insurance companies, pension funds and other investors, the money market would dry up very quickly, with very few lenders able to make new loans.

Federal Housing Administration (FHA)—A division within the Federal Department of Housing and Urban Development (HUD) that provides mortgage insurance—insuring the lender as to the borrower's ability to repay the debt for residential mortgages.

FHA Loan—A mortgage loan made by an approved lender, in which the loan is insured by the Federal Housing Administration.

Good Faith Estimate—A disclosure of estimated settlement costs. Federal regulations require that you receive this disclosure of estimated fees and other costs required to close the transaction within three days of your initial loan application.

Graduated Payment Mortgage (GPM)—A mortgage in which initial payments are lower for the first few years of the loan, but with increases on a regular basis, either annually or semiannually.

Growing Equity Mortgage (GEM)—A type of mortgage where payments increase yearly, and each increase is directly applied against the mortgage principal. This allows the borrowers to increase their equity quickly and pay the mortgage off sooner.

Housing-to-Income Ratio—The formula used by the loan officer to determine if a mortgage loan is within your income range. It compares your monthly mortgage expenses (Principal payment, Interest, Taxes and Insurance, hence known as PITI) to your gross monthly income. It is often referred to as the Front or Top ratio.

Liability—A liability is an outstanding debt such as a credit card balance or a car loan. You are required to list all your liabilities when applying for a mortgage loan.

LTV—Loan to Value—This is the ratio between your loan amount and the lower of the appraised or purchase price of the property.

Mortgage—A conditional transfer of property (land, house, etc.) as security for a loan. The property remains in the possession of the borrower but may be claimed by the lender if the loan and interest are not paid according to the terms agreed upon.

Mortgage Broker—A real estate financing professional who assists the buyer with the arrangement for mortgage financing.

Mortgage Insurance—This insurance is required if your down payment falls below a certain percentage, usually 20 percent. You would be required to pay a fee, which becomes part of your monthly mortgage payment, for this insurance which protects the lender should you default on the mortgage. On non-FHA loans, the payment for this insurance should be discontinued after the LTV drops below 80 percent of the appraised value.

Mortgage Note—A promissory note that you sign at closing which states your pledge to pay a specified amount at a set interest rate within a fixed period of time.

Mortgagee—A creditor, i.e., the lender.

Mortgagor—The debtor (borrower).

Origination—The completion of a loan application, which details your financial position and begins the mortgage loan process. As part of this first step, you may be required to provide past W2s, pay stubs and other supporting documentation of your income. Within three days, your loan officer must provide you with a Good Faith Estimate and a Truth-in-Lending disclosure, the latter commonly referred to as the REG-Z, as detailed by the Federal Reserve Bank's regulations.

Points—The fee (usually expressed as a percentage of the loan amount) charged by the originator, i.e., mortgage broker, banker, or lender. It's also called the origination fee. The points charged will vary with the loan amount and interest rate selected by the borrower.

Prequalification—The process that determines your ability to qualify for a mortgage loan based upon the amount of the loan, interest rate, term of the loan, and your income.

Principal—The outstanding balance owed on a loan, excluding interest due. Also, the amount in each payment which is applied to your mortgage balance.

Private Mortgage Insurance (PMI)—If your down payment is less than 20 percent, you may be required to pay PMI—a fee for mortgage insurance. This insurance, provided by a private mortgage insurance company, protects the lender should you default on your mortgage payments. However, the insurance covers only the difference between 80 percent of the original loan amount and the actual balance; I.e., if your loan is for 90 percent of the purchase prices, this insurance would apply only to the difference between the 90 percent loan and an 80 percent figure.

Processing—Following origination, the process carried out by the mortgage company verifying the information provided on your loan application. This includes ordering appraisals, credit reports and other documentation required for loan approval.

Recording Fees—The escrow office (or the attorney) who closes the transaction charges this fee, which covers fees charged to them by the recording office for officially recording the executed mortgage documents, which makes them of public record.

Servicing—overall term for the services the lender, or other company, provides in handling your mortgage payments. This includes collecting your payments, paying taxes and insurance if you have funds in an escrow or impound account. Frequently, the servicer is another company, unrelated to your original lender, who has acquired these rights from the owners of your mortgage to service the loan.

SubPrime Lenders—They used to be common in the premortgage meltdown era. No lenders are currently offering these loans. Many loans were made which did not meet Fannie Mae or Freddie Mac guidelines. The so-called "subprime" lenders made these loan, usually at a higher interest rate, to compensate the investor for the added risk of the loan.

These risks turned out to be well founded, Many lenders who made these loans are no longer in business. The loans were usually sold to investors as a security through some of the large financial houses on Wall Street. Like mortgages acquired by Fannie Mae and Freddie Mac, these loans may well wind up being held by insurance companies, pension funds and other investors.

Many of such loans wound up being syndicated and sold to investors overseas. Requirements on ratios, credit scores and other factors were considerably more lenient than with the typical Fannie Mae or Freddie Mac loan.

Title—Often called the deed. This is the document that evidences legal ownership of a specific property.

Title Insurance—An insurance policy which insures the purchaser against any errors in the title search (see definition below). This fee is part of the closing costs. If the insurer, for example, fails to discover a recorded lien on the property during their title search and subsequently insures the title as free and clear of any liens, the insurance company would have to pay that lien off at its own expense. Hence, the term, "title insurance."

Title Search—The process of examining the public records of a property. This is an official examination of public records by the title insurance company to determine legal ownership of the property and what liens may exist against that property. This is a necessary function that a lender will insist upon when they are expected to advance the funds for the mortgage.

Total Debt-to-Income Ratio—A formula used by a loan officer to determine if a mortgage loan is within your monthly income range. This ratio compares all your monthly debt payments, mortgage payments (principal and interest), taxes, insurance, credit cards, car payments and other similar payments to your monthly gross (pretax) income. Usually, total debt payments should be no more than 36 to 38 percent of your monthly income.

Underwriting—After processing, the documents in your loan file are evaluated by the lender to determine if the requested loan should be approved, denied, or perhaps approved with conditions.

VA Loan—A long-term, low or zero down payment mortgage loan that is guaranteed by the Veteran's Administration. Only veterans are eligible for this type of loan. The government guarantee is restricted to a certain percentage of the loan, which is sufficient to make it attractive to a lender.